QUILTS with Attitude

Deb Karasik

W9-AXE-182

Located in Paducah, Kentucky, the American Quilter's Society (AQS) is dedicated to promoting the accomplishments of today's quilters. Through its publications and events, AQS strives to honor today's quiltmakers and their work and to inspire future creativity and innovation in quiltmaking.

Text © 2009, Author, Deb Karasik
Artwork © 2009, American Quilter's Society

Executive Editor: Andi Milam Reynolds
Editor: Linda Baxter Lasco
Graphic Design: Barry Buchanan
Cover Design: Michael Buckingham
Photography: Charles R. Lynch
How-to Photography: Jeff Karasik

Additional copies of this book may be ordered from the American Quilter's Society, PO Box 3290, Paducah, KY 42002-3290, or online at www.AmericanQuilter.com.

All rights reserved. No part of this book may be reproduced, stored in any retrieval system, or transmitted in any form, or by any means including but not limited to electronic, mechanical, photocopy, recording, or otherwise, without the written consent of the author and publisher. Patterns may be copied for personal use only. While every effort has been made to ensure that the contents of this publication are as accurate and correct as possible, no warranty is provided nor results guaranteed. Since the author and AQS have no control over individual skills or choice of materials and tools, they do not assume responsibility for the use of this information.

Attention Photocopying Service–Please note the following: Publisher and author give permission to photocopy page 24.

Proudly printed and bound in the United States of America

Library of Congress Cataloging-in-Publication Data

Karasik, Deb.
  Quilts with attitude / by Deb Karasik.
    p. cm.
  ISBN 978-1-57432-966-7
  1. Patchwork. 2. Machine quilting. I. Title.

TT835.K379 2009
746.46--dc22
                                        2008047926

American Quilter's Society
P. O. Box 3290 • Paducah, KY 42002-3290
www.AmericanQuilter.com

DEDICATION

When I seriously started quilting in late 2000, I had no inkling that this journey would take me to where it has—and for that, I count my blessings each and every day. To thank all the individuals instrumental in my career, I would need a thousand pages, but since we don't have quite that much room, I'll cut to the chase and try to narrow it down a bit.

First, to both of my daughters, who constantly remind me that "young" is a state of mind, in no particular order:

For her courage, fortitude, and continued sense of humor, I thank my daughter Lauren for showing me that we can ALL face whatever life dishes out and keep our smiles intact.

To my daughter Sarah, thanks for showing me that no matter how far down one can get from life's adversities, we can hold our heads up proudly and laugh in the face of it all.

To my nieces, Shira and Tanya, I owe them volumes for showing me what true courage is. Without it, we are lost.

To my husband, Jeff, thank you for the thirty-five years of laughter, tears, sharing, hoping, dreaming, and continued encouragement.

And of course, I couldn't even think about being here if it weren't for Janet Mednick, my partner in quilting who coauthored *QuiltMavens: Perfect Paper Piecing* with me. She remains my friend and mentor in her quiet, eloquent way. Thank you, Janet.

Finally, I want to thank my dear friend Deborah Drescher for never ceasing to make me laugh!

For everyone else, and you know who you are, thank you all for the joy you share, the hope you spread, and the continued creative sparks you enable me to tap into!

Deb

ACKNOWLEDGMENTS

Just a simple thank you seems so inadequate, but I really do want to thank the following folks with heartfelt sincerity.

For those truly luscious fabrics that make up all of my quilts:
Bali Batiks (Princess Mirah)
Benartex
Free Spirit
Hoffman of California
Island Batiks
Robert Kaufman
Timeless Treasures

For my favorite sewing machine ever!!!
Brother International Corporation

For the most amazing quilting setup on the planet:
Handi Quilter Company & the HQ Sixteen machine

The most delicious threads ever:
WonderFil threads
Superior threads

Batting that's second to none:
Hobbs Bonded Fibers

THE perfect quilt design program:
Electric Quilt

The epitome of the perfect ruler:
CM Designs, Inc., for their Add-A-Quarter™ rulers

Thank you one and all for your continued support on this journey of a lifetime! I couldn't have done it without each and every one of you!

Deb

CONTENTS

CHAPTER 1

THE PROCESS: THE BIRTH OF INNER LIGHT

In this chapter I want to familiarize you with the basic process of quilt design, fabric and color choices, and the actual process of block and quilt assembly. Consider this your reference chapter and feel free to come back to it to refresh yourself with the techniques as you tackle the projects in the book.

Keep in mind, we all have different ways of working through these, but the steps I take have enabled me to complete my quilts pretty rapidly and precisely. For me, that's essential; my mind is constantly three to four quilts ahead of what I'm actually working on!

Most importantly... HAVE FUN!!!

THE PROCESS

When I teach or lecture, the number one question that I'm asked is, "How do you do it?" Now, that can certainly mean a lot of different things, but I try to answer based on how I get inspired and how I translate my ideas into quilts.

My inspiration comes from everything around me—architecture, nature, people, animals, events in my life. You name it, I'm inspired. Sometimes I just see a shape that's intriguing and I want to figure out how to incorporate it into a quilt. Other times, I'm just playing on my Electric Quilt® program and a quilt appears. There is just no one simple answer.

I tend to go through spurts of inspiration, in that I will design a half dozen to a dozen quilts, then make maybe one or two of them. It's an ongoing process and always subject to change. The number one thing I don't ever allow myself is to get discouraged. It's not a race; it's not going to be the end of the world if my quilts aren't so amazing that folks stop to catch their breath when they look at them!

I have learned to be less critical of my work. Sounds silly, but it's very freeing. Once you let go of all the self-recrimination, the creativity will flow much more freely and easily. Really!

OK, now let's say I have a design I want to tackle. How do I choose fabrics? It's a lot easier than it seems. I tend to go through favorites in my color choices. What I mean by that is, at some times I adore bright, crisp colors arranged in psychedelic canvases; other times I simply adore fall colors. I've even been known to work in pastels. But they're all wonderful, so how do I choose?

My selection process always starts the same way. I color in my designs in EQ6 with the fabrics and colors of the program (many of which I have downloaded) until I'm pleased with the overall look.

Do I always stick with the design? Absolutely not. When I go back through my quilts and see how I have colored them in EQ as compared to the actual quilts, it always makes me chuckle. I rarely stick with the color palette I originally designed; here's why.

I print out my line drawing and my colored version from EQ and slap them up on the design wall. Then I start pulling fabrics. For some reason, I will always start at the center of the quilt and work my way outwards. Is this right or wrong? I have no idea, nor do I care. I do what feels right for me. I encourage you to do the same.

At any given moment, I'll have a favorite fabric. You surely have one, too. It's the one you don't want to cut into! That's the one I pull first. I pin a chunk up on the design wall and stare at it. Will it end up in the quilt? There's only a 50-50 chance. Just because I adore it doesn't mean it's right for the quilt. Then I start pulling other fabrics I adore. I don't think about color rules; I believe there are none. I don't think about pattern yet. I'm all for feeling, not thinking, about my choices. I hope this makes sense to you.

Now there will be a plethora of colors and patterns staring back at me, and usually they make no sense at first. I let my chunks sit on my design wall, sometimes for days, before I start making final selections. Sometimes I know immediately if they're right or wrong for my quilt and sometimes I don't. But I can assure you; the fabrics that are right WILL make themselves known.

Here's a good example of what I'm talking about.

This is my original EQ rendition of NAPA VALLEY SUNSET (fig. 1).

Fig. 1. NAPA VALLEY SUNSET original

This is how it turned out (fig. 2).

Fig. 2. NAPA VALLEY SUNSET, 80" x 80", made by the author. Pattern is available in *QuiltMavens: Perfect Paper Piecing* by Deb Karasik and Janet Mednick (AQS, 2007).

Not exactly what I started with, but it's OK! To me, this is the most exciting part of the design process.

With spikey quilts, besides all the color/pattern choices, you also have to be cognizant of the contrast. In order for the spikes to show up well, there has to be contrast, consistent throughout the quilt.

I test contrast by lining up touching colors. If I can't see a crisp line between them, they don't work. They may look nice together, but why go to all the work of making a zillion spikes only to have them disappear in the fabric? I don't think so.

In this example it's easy to see the spikes against the background fabric (fig. 3).

Fig. 3.

In this example, the spikes disappear into the background fabric (fig. 4).

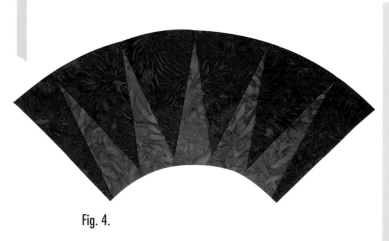

Fig. 4.

Subtle changes in the fabrics can make all the difference with these quilts. This is usually the point where my favorite fabric is folded up and put back into the stash closet. It looks awesome WITH the other fabrics, but doesn't allow for good contrast. C'est la vie. I will use it in another quilt down the road.

Once basic colors are chosen, again I'm drawn to the center of the quilt and start building from there. If I get frustrated or colors just aren't working for me, I walk away from it, work on another project, or leave the room. It really works.

Sometimes we just think too hard. Yes, we're all guilty of it—you know you are too! If we walk away from a project and come back to it another day, it's amazing what a different light we see it in. Don't beat yourself up for not "getting it" all at once. Our brains need time to process. This is all part of the design process. With the attention span of a gnat, I need to constantly remind myself of this. My mantra should be "slow down."

That's my basic process. I can't say it's instinctive and comes naturally to me, because it doesn't always. Yes, there are some quilts, complete with color, that are in my head and do become quilts, but not many. I get about one or two of those a year. For the most part though, I work through this process.

I learned a long time ago that I'm not the creative genius behind my quilts. THEY are. They decide how they want to look; I'm just the stitcher.

Let your quilts speak to you. They will, you know, you just have to listen!

USING THE CD

All of the patterns are given on the enclosed CD as PDF files, which can be viewed in Preview or Acrobat. The link to download Acrobat is included on the CD. It makes it possible to print all the patterns from your computer's printer in the correct size, thus eliminating the trouble of copying and enlarging them from the pages of a book.

The CD is easy to use and features a pdf-based program that runs from Adobe Reader 5.0 or higher. If you don't already have this program on your computer, it is a free download from Adobe.com, or you can copy it from this CD.

If the patterns don't automatically open when you load your CD, open the file <AttitudePattern-index.pdf>. From this page, you should be able to open any foundation pattern by clicking on its thumbnail, or by clicking on its line on the contents page. If larger than 8½" x 11", the pattern will open in a separate multi-page document from which you can print the tiled pages for easy assembly. Control+P will open your print dialogue box, or you can click on the <print pattern> link. Make sure you indicate which page numbers you want to print before sending the file to the printer.

Thumbnail

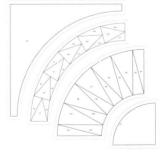
Foundations

CHOOSING THE PERFECT SETTING AND
MAKING IT EASY!

As any quilter will tell you, choosing a
setting can make or break the overall appearance
of a quilt. I've learned not to fear settings
because of their obvious complexity, but rather
embrace their challenge to create fun and
intricate quilts. However, not being the kind of
quilter who likes to spend months working on
a single quilt, I ALWAYS find a way to make
assembly easy, fun, and faster than ever before.
So let's start having some fun choosing a setting
for your perfect quilt!

Because I can't draw a straight line, I use
EQ6 software to design all of my quilts. The
program enables me to go through a large
number of settings and I can enhance them
in any way I see fit. Star patterns have always
intrigued me, but Y seams are not my favorite,
so I will do anything to avoid them. At first I
just design around them. Then I make changes
to eliminate them.

Let me take you through the design process.

Settings I choose are usually something like
these (figs. 5–10).

Fig. 6.

Fig. 7.

Fig. 5.

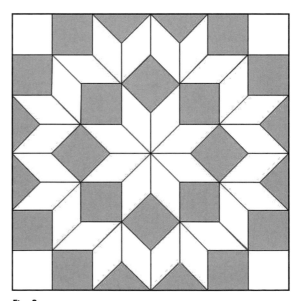

Fig. 8.

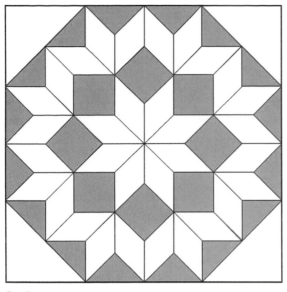

Fig. 9.

Fig. 10.

Let's start with the simplest setting and build our spikey quilt together.

The first thing we need to consider is what kind of block we want to drop into this setting. The blocks always start out as standard square blocks in EQ6. When they are dropped into a setting, they will adapt to the shape of the area they are dropped into.

For example, start with a block that looks like this (fig. 11).

Fig.11.

When you drop it into the star diamond setting it will take on a significantly different look. Rotating the block will also change the look. One way gives you more extreme curves to sew (fig. 12a). The other provides more gradual curves that are easier to sew (fig. 12b).

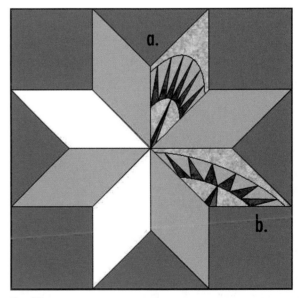

Fig. 12.

Do you see how exciting this can be? Sometimes the creative process can be as much fun as the actual sewing!

I always like to challenge myself a bit with my quilts, so double- or triple-row blocks please me the most (figs. 13–15).

Fig. 15. Triple-row block

Fig. 13. Double-row block

To keep this design fairly simple, we want to choose a block that will give us gradual curves when dropped into this setting. We'll start with the block below and see how it looks set into the star format (fig. 16).

Fig. 14. Double-row block

Fig. 16.

Let's change the colors and see how it changes shape in the star setting (fig. 17).

Fig. 17.

When the block is set into a diamond like this it's dramatic, but the tighter curves are a bit intimidating, so I think I'll try another setting (fig. 18).

Fig. 18.

This setting is a bit more interesting, as it now has some motion. See how your eye moves around the quilt, as if it were a moving pinwheel? This is one way to bring drama to the pattern while highlighting the fabrics at the same time.

Now try alternating the position of the design within the diamonds (fig. 19).

Fig. 19.

This setting is the one that sings to me. I see so many possibilities for fabric placement, and perhaps additional block placement around the outer areas, that I just can't resist it!

Learn to play with your design's rotation and placement and don't be impatient. This is when you need to take your time until you hit upon a quilt design that really looks interesting. In this example, the simple rotation gave three very different quilts.

Now I know what you're thinking. "Look at all the Y seams! How can that be easy?" Well, let's take care of that right now!

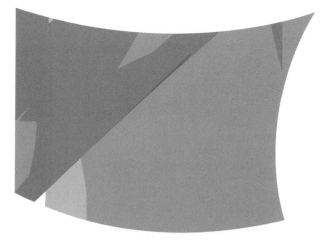

By carefully examining this layout, you can see that there are eight Y seams (fig. 20).

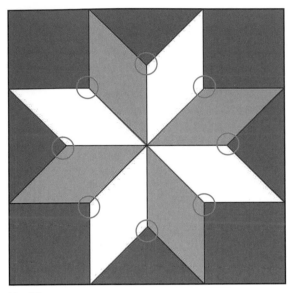

Fig. 20.

Being a fan of fast, easy, and accurate, I need to come up with block designs that enable me to avoid these set-in seams. Blocks that are split on the diagonal eliminate the Y seams, so I try to design blocks that can be assembled with a center diagonal seam (fig. 21).

Fig. 21.

Now we can design the blocks needed to fill in the outer areas. Once again, there are choices to make. Should the blocks surrounding the star be the same or will different ones be more interesting? Don't be afraid to play with different blocks as you go through your design process.

Notice that the blocks at the top, bottom, and sides of the star are only half of a square, and that half-square needs to have a center seam (figs. 22–23).

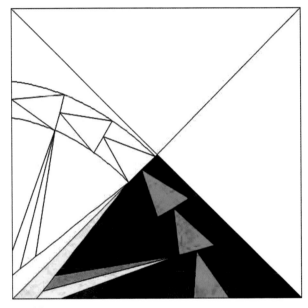

Fig. 22.

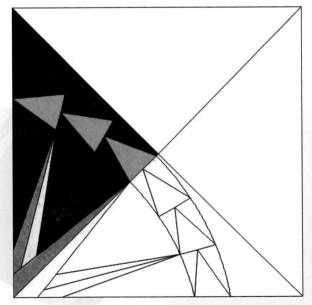

Fig. 23.

Sewn together they look like this (fig. 24).

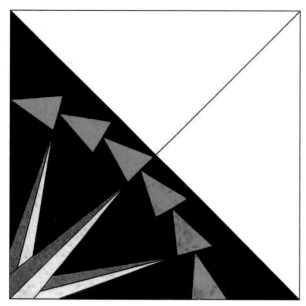

Fig. 24.

Let's see what happens when they are dropped into the quilt. The half-square blocks add wonderful dimension and interest to the quilt (fig. 25).

Fig. 25.

But it's still not done! Let's try setting these same blocks in a full-square block at the corners and see what happens.

Now this basic diamond setting, once rather plain, has become a multidimensional quilt design with sparkle and glow! And the best part is that the assembly will be fast and easy! (fig. 26).

Fig. 26.

Everyone works in their own way. In my case, I make the quilt tops first and put them on the design wall for a few days or even a few weeks before a border design comes to me. So, let's get to work on this quilt and leave the border(s) for later.

Inner Light, 44" x 44", made by the author

COLOR, COLOR, COLOR

Color is the most personal part of any quilt for me. All of us tend to use colors that please us and hopefully work well in the quilts we make. We all have our favorites, but are they always used successfully? Speaking for myself, I know I've made some questionable color choices in my past quilts. Working with spikes has taught me the importance of contrast, to appreciate gradations of color, and to work with colors I'm not particularly comfortable with.

I wanted the quilt we're designing to glow, either in the center or at the edges. The only logical way to achieve this was to try gradations of color. You can use either fabrics that are solid (or read as solid, like Bali batiks) or small-scale prints. Try to avoid large-scale patterns as the colors could fall in the wrong places and the spikes will look wonky. As you can see, the glow goes from the center outward.

Spikey quilts require a great deal of contrast as well as careful color placement to enhance the design. Although it may sound daunting, it's really easy once you learn the basics.

If you're using color gradations to enhance your quilt, start with your first gradation and build from that. In this case, let's start with the background of the center spikes.

I used a variety of blues to obtain the glow I was seeking. See how they're lighter in the center and work out toward the edge ending in a dark blue? The effect is reinforced in the outer ring of spikes with the use of yellows to reds. But in order for this to work, you have to be very cognizant of the spike colors—where the backgrounds are light, the spikes must be dark, and vice versa (fig. 27).

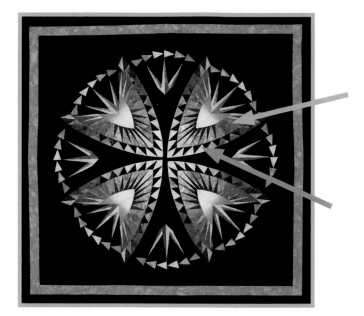

Fig 27. INNER LIGHT

In the blue background, I wanted a spike color that was subtle but showed up well against the blue. I chose pinks and purples, carefully placing them where there would be the most contrast. I am proud of my spikes and want them to show up clearly, no matter what part of the block they're in.

For the outer ring, I chose a contrasting selection of purples to stand out against the yellows and reds. It's subtle, but it works wonderfully against the deep black overall background of the quilt.

Now watch what happens when you start to tweak the colors.

This is the original with the background in black (fig. 28).

Fig. 28.

Look what happens with a change in colors and background. It's a completely different looking quilt (fig. 29).

Fig. 29.

Fig. 30.

If you decide you don't want the gradations style, you can still get a beautiful quilt (fig. 30).

Color is your friend. Don't be afraid to play with the endless possibilities of color combinations. Pull colors you don't particularly care for and throw in fabrics and colors you love. All of a sudden those "uglies" become welcome additions to your quilts.

Most importantly, have fun. We sew and quilt because we love this amazing art form, so that when we stop having fun, it's over. So find your happy sewing place, your particular comfort zone, and then start breaking the rules.

SEWING THE BLOCKS

For those of you out there who love the look of paper-pieced quilts but find the process a bit daunting, I can assure you, it's not. Can you sew a straight line? OK then, you're almost there!

The paper piecing process I use, for every paper-piecing project I do, is the QuiltMavens' Perfect Paper Piecing method. It's fast, easy, and takes the stress out of foundation piecing that plagues so many quilters.

Follow the process for this fairly intricate design, then get started with some of the beginning projects that come next.

There are only two basic blocks in this quilt, so let's start with the center block (fig. 31).

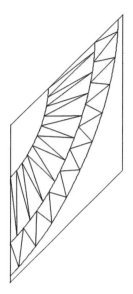

Fig. 31.

I start by printing out the foundations from the companion CD. Please note that the outer spikey arcs range from B1 to B21.

There are eight center blocks, four with the gradations of color going from light to dark and four with color gradations going from dark to light.

I precut the fabric for the paper piecing, each piece at least 1"–1¹/₂" longer and wider than the area it will cover. Then I stack the cut pieces in the order they are going to be sewn, starting with the first background piece (fig. 32).

Fig. 32.

I pick up my first two pieces and remember this one, VERY important rule (which I will repeat to death).

The back of the background fabric is the first thing to touch the back of the paper!

Sound silly? Well, think about it. Starting the block is the trickiest part of paper piecing. Really! If you can commit this little saying to memory (and I will make sure you do!), it will absolutely save you time and ripping.

So remember, the back of the background fabric is the first thing to touch the back of the paper!

With the fabric right sides together, I line up the first two pieces approximately ¹/₄" past the first sewing line (fig. 33a).

Transparent paper, such as QuiltMavens' Perfect Paper Piecing Paper, eliminates the need to hold it up to the light for placement. See the Resources page on how to get some for yourself (fig. 33b).

Fig. 33.

With a small stitch length (set between 1.0 and 1.5), start sewing at the outer cutting line, along the seam line between #1 and #2, and end at the opposite outer cutting line (fig. 34).

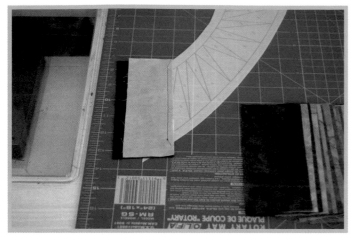

Fig. 34.

Flip the paper over. Open out the piece to cover area #2 and press. I use a wooden seam roller; I never have to plug it in and, most importantly, I don't burn myself (fig. 35)!

Fig. 35.

Flip the paper back over and place a hard edge tool (I recommend using a piece of template plastic) exactly on the *next* sewing line, between pieces #2 and #3 (fig. 36).

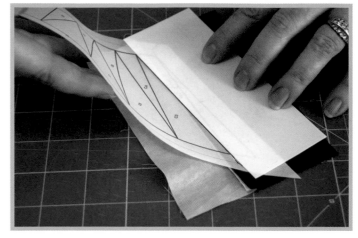

Fig. 36.

Fold the paper back over the hard edge tool (fig. 37).

Fig. 37.

Place the lip of an Add-A-Quarter ruler right up next to the folded paper.

Trim away the excess fabric with a rotary cutter (fig. 38).

Fig. 38.

You now have a perfect ¼" seam (fig. 39)!

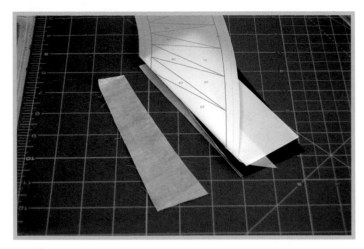

Fig. 39.

Unfold the paper. Take a piece of fabric from the next pile (it should be a background color) and align it with the just-trimmed edge, right sides together. Turn the paper over, sew along the line between #2 and #3, and press with the seam roller (fig. 40). Fold the paper and trim as before.

Fig. 40.

You will very quickly develop a comfortable rhythm doing this. When you finish the piecing, trim away the excess fabric along the outer cutting line. Leave the paper on and set aside (fig. 41).

After piecing all the spikey units, it's time for the background pieces.

Starch the fabric for the background pieces. I can't stress enough how much it will make a difference. The starch will stabilize the bias edges and make them easier to handle during assembly.

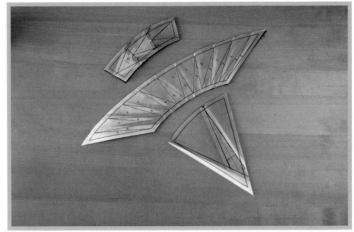

Fig. 41.

My favorite starch is Mary Ellen's Best Press. It does the job well with no flaking. I think it's simply the best and it has an awesome smell. I prefer Caribbean Beach, but it's also available without any scent. (If you have to starch, you might as well enjoy it!)

But I digress. Use the templates to cut out the background pieces (which are usually arcs).

Here's what I call the three-pin method of joining curved seams.

With the paper still on, fold the outer spikey unit in half to find the center. Pinch press a fold here or mark it with a pin (fig. 42).

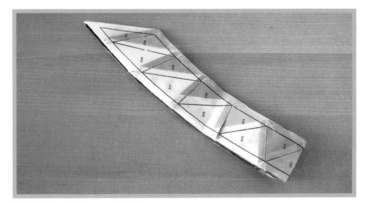

Fig. 42.

Fold the outside arc unit in half and pinch press a fold at the center (fig. 43).

Fig. 43.

Line up the centers of the two pieces, right sides together, and pin them. Place two more pins, one at either edge as shown (fig. 44).

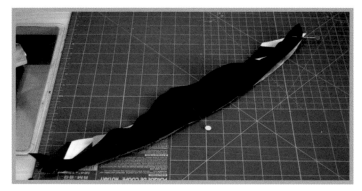

Fig. 44.

Gently ease in the curved seam. I ALWAYS sew with the paper down, fabric up. It makes no difference if I'm sewing a concave curve on top or a convex curve on top.

If the fabric is on the bottom, you will get bunching, puckers, and overall icky spots. Trust me on this one. I may not have the scientific explanation, but I've set in enough of these units to consider myself something of an expert!

Press the seam allowance toward the background piece and set aside (fig. 45).

In the same way, join the inner spikey units with the inside arcs, using the three-pin method and sewing with the paper down, fabric up.

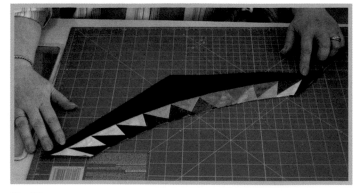

Fig. 45.

Remove the paper from the outer spikey units (shown in yellows and purples). Fold an outer and inner spikey unit in half to find the centers. Line up, pin as before, and ease the two spikey units together. If it is easier for you, you can pin more frequently than just the three pins we used before.

Remove the paper from the inner spikey units and press.

Voila! The blocks look great, don't they?

The quilt is assembled in 8 sections. Since we divided the outer blocks in half, there are no Y-seams (set-in seams) to worry about.

Join the 3 units of each section, then join the 8 sections to complete the quilt top (fig. 46).

Make several copies of page 24 to choose colors for your own version of INNER LIGHT (fig. 51). Pull fabric from your stash and jump in.

Yardage

These are the foundations (figs. 47–50) and yardage you'll need. Pull fabrics from your stash for the spikes.

4 yards quilt background (shown in black)
⅛ yard of each of 11 colors for inner block background (shown in gradations of blue)
⅛ yard of each of 10 colors for spikes (shown in gradations of pinks)
⅛ yard of each of 11 colors for outer ring block backgrounds (shown in red to yellow)

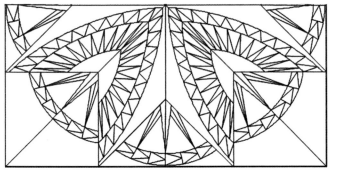

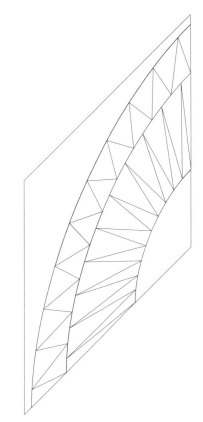

Fig. 46.

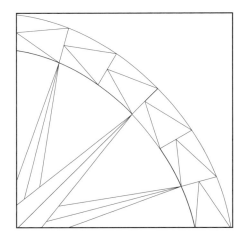

Fig. 48. Print 8 light_center blk.pdf

⅛ yard of each of 10 colors for outer ring spikes (shown in gradations of purple)

½ – ¾ yard of a gradation fabric for inner block inside arcs (shown in yellow/orange)

⅛ yard of each of 3 colors for Flying Geese (shown in blue)

¼ yard of each of 2 colors for inner arc split spikes

½ yard inner border (shown in turquoise)

3 yards backing

52" x 52" batting

Foundations

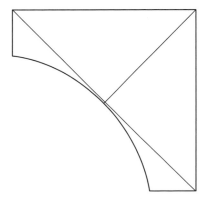

Fig. 49. Print 8 light_spikeygeese.pdf

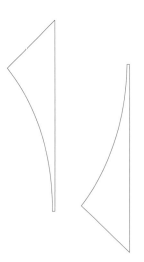

Fig. 50. Print 4 light_large_arc.pdf

Fig. 47. Print 4 light_small_arc.pdf

Fig. 51. Color your own version of INNER LIGHT. You can change the orientation of the quilt by the placement of the Spikey Geese blocks.

CHAPTER 2
STARTING SIMPLE

Let's start with a couple of really simple projects that will not only get you past the trepidation of paper piecing, but also will get you warmed up for the more intricate projects. These projects provide a quick and easy way to familiarize yourself with paper piecing.

I chose projects that are just as nice to keep as they are to give as gifts. So pull yourself up to your sewing machine and let's have some fun!

PERFECT PLACEMAT

14" x 20", made by the author

"LET'S GET
STARTED"
PROJECTS

See the Tools section for a discussion on the different kinds of foundation paper and the kind I prefer to use (page 92).

Just to get your feet wet, let's start with a very simple placemat. Of course, you're going to want to make dozens of them, but let's just start with one.

The placemat is actually just four blocks put together (figs. 1–2). When you see the blocks like this, they're a lot less intimidating, aren't they? Well, that's what paper piecing is all about. You get complex looking quilts, much easier than you thought possible.

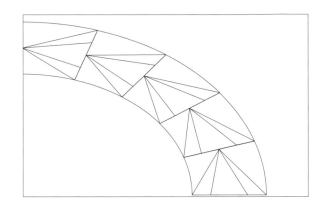

Fig. 2. Print 2 placemat_b.pdf

Chicken Feet Cutting Chart

PLACEMENT	COLOR	PIECES NEEDED	SIZE OF EACH PIECE
chicken feet	dark	40	$1\frac{1}{2}$" x 4"
background	light	60	$2\frac{1}{2}$" x 4"

Starch the background yardage with Mary Ellen's Best Press for ease of handling during assembly. Use the F and G templates to cut out the remaining pieces.

Yardage for One Placemat

1 fat quarter for inside arcs
1 fat quarter for chicken feet
½ yard for chicken feet background
1 fat quarter for outside arcs
⅜ yard binding
⅔ yard backing
18" x 24" batting

Sewing Sequence

We'll start with block A and piece the chicken feet first. Make sure you pay attention to the lettered sequence of these chicken feet. Because of the elongated block, it DOES matter in what order they are placed.

Foundations

I lay out my fabrics in the order they're going to be sewn. We'll need the background rectangles stacked nicely next to the chicken feet fabrics. It's much easier to just grab and sew than to have to stop and think between each seam. I'm all for the easy way!

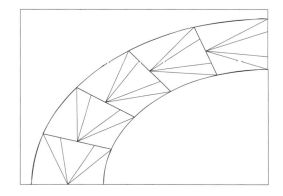

Fig. 1. Print 2 placemat_a.pdf

To keep the separate chicken feet units in order, piece the A unit and set it aside. Piece the B unit and sew it onto the A unit, and so on. As you finish each subsequent unit, join it with the completed units. This way they are pieced and sewn together in order as you go along. No worry about pieces getting lost or mixed up. (I hate ripping seams, especially when they're tiny little stitches like these!)

So, pick up your first chicken feet foundation (A) and remember, *the back of the background fabric is the first thing to touch the back of the paper!*

Place one background piece and one chicken toe piece, right sides together, and line up their edges approximately ¼" past the sewing line between A1 and A2, positioning them on the unprinted side of the paper.

Set the stitch length between 1.0 and 1.5. With the printed side facing you and the fabric underneath, sew from the outer cutting line, along the seam line, to the opposite outer cutting line.

Turn the paper over, flip the top fabric open to cover the A2 space, and press the seam. I recommend using a wooden seam roller. You never have to plug it in and, most importantly, you won't burn yourself.

Turn the foundation back over. Place the straight edge of a hard edge tool (I use template plastic) directly on the *next* sewing line (between A2 and A3). Fold the paper back along that line.

Place an Add-A-Quarter ruler right up next to the folded paper and trim away the excess fabric using a sharp rotary cutter.

Take the next piece of background fabric and line it up with the trimmed edge, right sides together. Turn the foundation over and sew from one outer cutting line to the other.

Turn over, flip open the background piece just sewn, and press.

Fold the paper at the next sewing line (between A3 and A4), trim, align the next piece of fabric (chicken toe again), and sew as before.

Continue in this manner until the unit is complete.

When you have finished piecing the unit, trim along the outer cutting line, cutting off any excess fabric beyond the cutting line. *Leave the paper on* and set aside.

Piece the second chicken feet unit, join with the first, and so on until all five chicken feet units (A–E) are complete.

Use the three-pin method (pages 21–22) to add the inside and outside arcs, remembering to sew with the paper side down. (You'll notice I decided on an oval placemat and eliminated the outside arc.)

Press the seam allowance toward the arcs.

Remove the paper to complete block A.

In the same way, make the second block A and two of block B.

Assemble them as shown, and voilà! You have your first placemat top (fig. 3, page 29).

For quilting, I wanted a stability and kind of flatness in the center where the plates will go, so I did a meander with about ½" between the quilting lines.

The chicken feet detail on page 29 shows a simple quilting design to let the spikes shine, not the quilting. Of course, this was my choice and these are YOUR placemats, so have fun with any kind of quilting that makes you happy.

Are you addicted to spikes yet? Not quite? Well, keep going, because I guarantee by the end of this book you will crave spikes as much as those who love them crave potato chips!

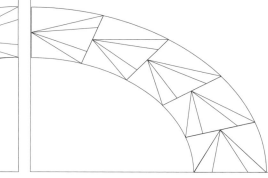

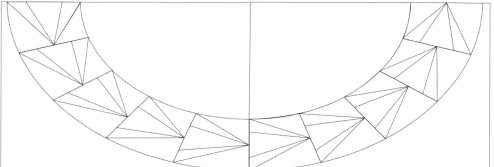

Fig. 3. Placemat assembly

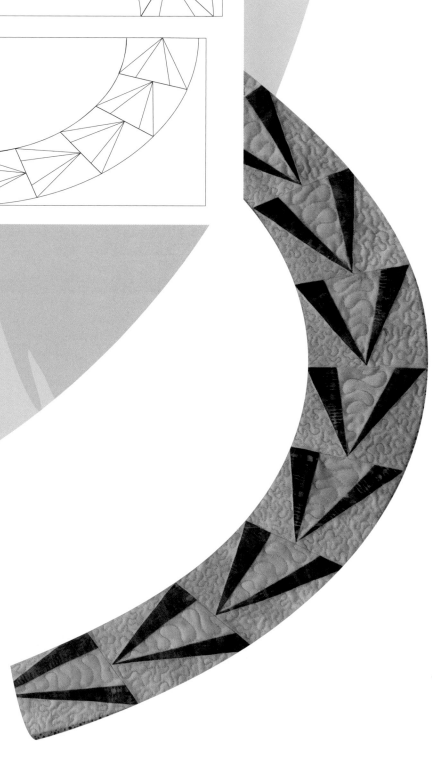

TERIFFIC TABLE TOPPER

32" x 44", made by the author

When I finished with my placemats, I knew I had to either make a table runner or table topper to match them. This is probably backwards thinking, but welcome to my world. Anyway, I went and stared at my dining room table and decided I really needed an oval. Why? Because that's the shape of my table! I also didn't want anything that covered the top entirely as I really love the wood of my table and wanted to see it, even with a topper in place. Once again, it's probably not conventional thinking, but I've never been thought of as conventional anyway, so why start now?

The topper is divided into four sections: the inner compass spikey block, a plain arc with no piecing, an arc of chicken feet, and an optional outside arc border (as with the placemat, omit it if you want an oval; add it if you want a rectangle).

Yardage

½ yard dark for compass spikes
½ yard medium for compass spikes
⅔ yard for the compass background
1 yard for the outside arc border (optional)
1½ yards chicken feet background
⅔ yard print for chicken feet
1 yard for the plain inside arc
⅜ yard binding
1⅜ yard backing
38" x 50" batting

Foundations
See figures 1 – 4.

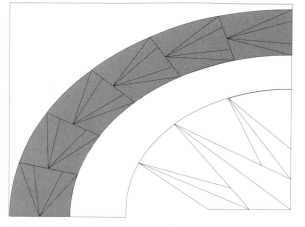
Fig. 1. Print 2 topper_compass_a.pdf

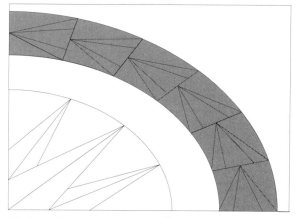
Fig. 2. Print 2 topper_compass_b.pdf

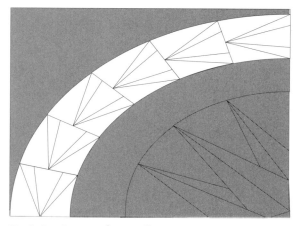
Fig. 3. Print 2 topper_feet_a.pdf

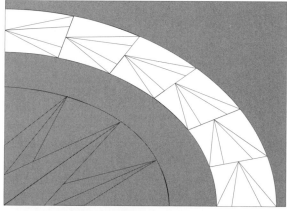
Fig. 4. Print 2 topper_feet_b.pdf

Center Compass Cutting Chart

PLACEMENT	COLOR	PIECES NEEDED	SIZE OF EACH PIECE
A1	dark	2	9" x 2½"
A2	medium	2	9" x 2½"
A3 & B4	background	4	9" x 5"
A4 & B3	background	4	8" x 5"
A5	medium	2	12" x 3"
B1	dark	2	10½" x 2½"
B2	medium	2	10½" x 2½"
B5	dark	2	12" x 3"

Chicken Feet Cutting Chart

PLACEMENT	COLOR	PIECES NEEDED	SIZE OF EACH PIECE
chicken feet	dark	48	6" x 3½"
background	light	72	6" x 2"

Starch the background yardage and cut out the arcs using the C, CR and J, JR templates.

Sewing Sequence

When I'm working on a project, I do all the paper piecing units first before moving on to assembling any of the blocks. I call it "doing the hard stuff first." This is how I like to reward myself throughout the quiltmaking process—by doing the hard stuff first, then coasting through the easy stuff. It works for me. Laugh if you want, but I don't have *any* UFOs!

On the topper, I recommend starting with the center compass unit, then doing the chicken feet arc.

Paper piece 4 center compass units.

Paper piece 4 chicken feet arcs.

Start with the sewing line between 1 & 2, and line up your fabrics just as you did before. Remember, the back of the background fabric is the first thing to touch the back of the paper! (I warned you that I was going to keep repeating this until you got it. Don't be surprised when it shows up again!)

TIP: When sewing longer spikes, pin them to the paper to keep them from slipping while you sew.

Assembly

Join the plain inside arcs (C and CR) and the chicken feet arcs. Press the seam allowances away from the paper-pieced units.

Add the inner compass units, then the optional outside border (J and JR).

Join the four sections to complete the topper.

Quilting

The background quilting detail features a meander, partly because I wanted to have consistency between the placemats and the topper and partly because it will make the topper lie flat. But the main reason was because I really like to meander.

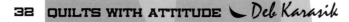

CHAPTER 3
THE ZEN OF IT ALL

Ever have those moments when you wished you were sitting on the beach of a tropical island, totally alone? We all get them once in a while, and for some of us, it's easy to escape the everyday trials and tribulations. For others, it's not so easy.

Zen, as it was explained to me, is the enlightenment brought about by understanding and knowledge. It can also mean an inner peace that enables us to reach this enlightenment. For me, the latter is my Zen, especially the inner peace part. Being calm does not come naturally to me.

When I was designing the next three quilts, each with its own little story, the one thread they all have in common is that they are peaceful. I hope they work that way for you as well.

We all have trials in our lives that challenge us, and the Karasik family is no different. I found that these little quilts helped me find my calm place, my inner peace as it were. I found them relaxing to make and even more soothing to look at, so I thought I'd share them with you. Maybe you will find the same calm that I did, and if so, YAY! (Oh, and you won't have to sit on the floor cross-legged to make these!)

HARVEST MOON

24" x 24", made by the author

This is
the first quilt
in my Zen series.
In 2007, there were
horrific fires all over
southern California. Due
to their size and the weeks the
fires dragged on, the smoke came
up to northern California as well.
One evening, my husband and I were
driving by the beach and saw a HUGE
full moon that was coppery, orange, and
gold—the result of the smoke in the air. I
knew then I had to make it into a quilt.

I chose to make my moon using the colors
I saw in the sky, but it's also exquisite in other
colors—blues, purples, reds, or just about
anything you can dream of! I've made moons in
a lot of color and size combinations and they all
make me smile.

The moon is divided in half with an outside arc
added to each half before they're joined.

Yardage

19 strips 3" x 20" in a variety of fabrics for the moon
5/8 yard black for the background and borders
1 fat quarter for the contrasting borders and binding
1/4 yard binding
7/8 yard backing
28" x 28" batting

Foundations

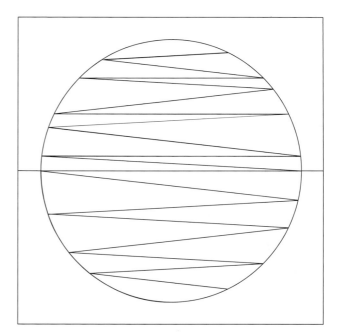

Fig. 1. Print 1 harvestmoon.pdf

Cutting

Cut border strips from the black background fabric.

4 strips 2" x 24"

Cut border strips from the contrasting fat quarter.

2 strips 1" x 22"
2 strips 2" x 22"
5 strips 1" x 22" for the binding

Starch the remaining black fabric and cut the two outside arcs (A and D) for the top and bottom halves of the quilt.

Sewing Sequence

Lay out your strips in the order you want to see them in the quilt, from B1 at the top of the moon through C8 at the bottom. Then stack them for easy grabbing while you sew (fig. 2).

Fig. 2.

Paper piece the two halves of the moon, starting with the first two strips, right sides together, and the back of the first piece up against the back of the paper.

Sew, press, and trim until all 19 strips have been used.

Assembly

The curve of the outside arcs looks extreme, but trust me, the arcs set in like a breeze. Apparently it knows its Zen (fig. 3).

Fig. 3.

Use the three-pin method. Sew with the paper-pieced unit down and ease in the arc unit to the moon unit. Repeat with the other half moon and arc. (I confess, on a long curve like this one, I'll use a couple of extra pins – fig. 4.)

Fig. 4.

With right sides together, sew the two completed moon halves together. Remove all the paper and press with a hot iron. I also starch again at this point but it's not necessary unless you're an avid starcher.

Add the borders with the wider strips in the first border on two adjacent sides and the wider black strips of the second border on the opposite adjacent sides as seen in the photo. Add a third border of same-size strips.

Quilting

Because of the simplicity of the pattern, I did a medium sized meander on the background and just a simple wavy line throughout the spikey moon units. I added a pebbly design on the border.

MIDNIGHT IN THE FOREST

26" x 26", made by the author

Here's another quilt from my Zen series. I really got hooked on the moon as a focal point as I find it very soothing. I hope you do as well.

This quilt was made entirely from my scraps. No pieces were larger than a couple inches wide (except for the black background, but those were scraps as well!). Then the outer spikey border was made entirely with random scraps left over from the moon and tree. Enough yardage is given for purchasing and precutting all your pieces, but if you utilize leftover scraps as I did, you'll need less.

I can't stress enough, that you should put in the fabrics and colors that please you. I chose these colors because they were already cut up and ready for piecing. I've since made this with a blue moon, a purple moon, and a hot pink moon. Remember, there are no rules to the creative process except to have fun.

Yardage

1¼ yards total mixed golds, oranges, and yellows for the moon and spikey border

1¼ yards total mixed greens for the tree and spikey border background

1 fat quarter dark for the background

1 scrap brown for the tree trunk

⅛ yard inner border

¼ yard binding

⅞ yard backing

30" x 30" batting

Foundations

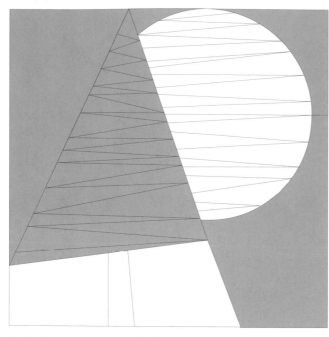

Fig. 1. Print 1 forest_moon_blk.pdf

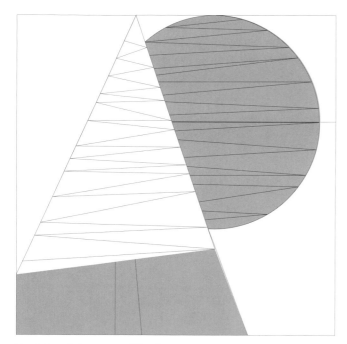

Fig. 2. Print 1 forest_tree_blk.pdf

Cutting Chart for Quilt Top

PLACEMENT	COLOR	PIECES NEEDED	SIZE OF EACH PIECE
moon	golds	22	$2\frac{1}{2}$" x 12"
tree	greens	25	$2\frac{1}{2}$" x 12"
C2	brown	1	$2\frac{1}{2}$" x $5\frac{1}{2}$"
C1	dark	1	5" x 6"
C3		1	5" x $6\frac{1}{2}$"

Use the F, G, H, and I templates to cut the remaining pieces from the background fabric. Starch the yardage for ease of handling during the quilt top assembly.

Sewing Sequence

Arrange the 22 moon pieces in the order they'll be sewn.

Paper piece the two moon sections (D and E).

Arrange the 25 tree pieces in the order they'll be sewn.

Paper piece the tree (A and B).

Paper piece the tree trunk and background unit (C).

Assembly

Add the G and H pieces to the top half of the moon.

Add the I piece to the bottom half of the moon, then join the two moon units.

Add the F triangle to the tree, then join with the trunk unit (C).

Join the tree and moon units to complete the top.

Square up to 17½" x 17½".

Cutting Chart for Border Blocks

PLACEMENT	COLOR	PIECES NEEDED	SIZE OF EACH PIECE
border spikes	golds	96	2½" x 3½"
border background	green	96	2½" x 3½"
corner block background	green	12	3" x 4"
inner border	contrast	4	1½" x 22"

Note: You may be able to collect two piles of all the little bitlets of leftovers from the moon and tree for the border and only need to cut the inner border strips.

Arrange the pieces for the spikey border unit and make 8 border units and 4 corner units.

Add the 1½" contrasting inner border strips to the completed top.

Join the border and corner units as shown and add to the 4 sides of quilt top (fig. 5).

Border Foundations

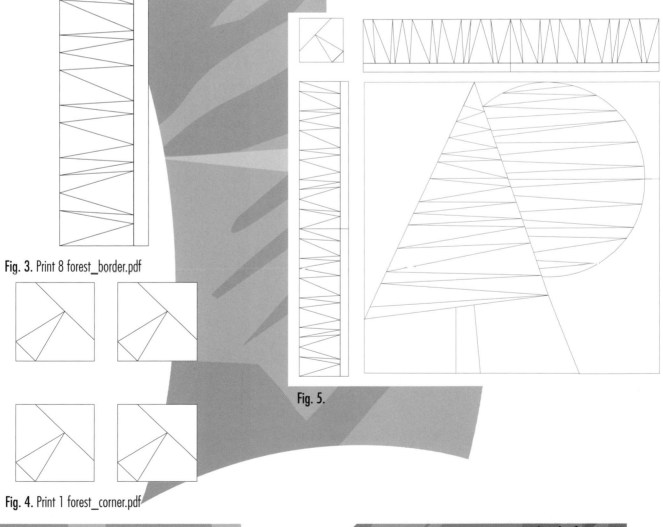

Fig. 3. Print 8 forest_border.pdf

Fig. 5.

Fig. 4. Print 1 forest_corner.pdf

Quilting

I chose to quilt the background black on black, but in retrospect, wouldn't a wonderful sparkly metallic be fun? Even if you quilt in stars here and there, a very different quilt would emerge. If you decide to keep it simple, like I did, you will still have a really wonderful quilt, perfect for keeping or gift giving!

SUNRISE OVER THE MOUNTAIN

22" x 22", made by Sandy McCause,
Spirit Lake, Idaho

A few years ago, I saw a quilt at a show with little Moon over the Mountain blocks and was intrigued by their simple beauty. But of course, there weren't any spikes and we can't have that now, can we?

So I played with the moon and decided a few, simple spikes would be all that was needed to jazz it up a bit. Wrong! The simple spikes looked kind of boring to me, so I gave them little points of their own.

And seriously, a triangle for the mountain? Surely we needed more than a simple triangle for our mountain. So I added spikes and I was much happier.

This delightful little wallhanging is a great way to familiarize yourself with spikes and curves without any stress at all! What could be better? So dig through your stash and pull some delicious sunrise type fabrics and let's get started.

Yardage

1 fat quarter for the center arcs (sun)
1 fat eighth for the spikes (medium)
1 fat eighth for the spike tips (dark)
½ yard background for spikes and outside arcs (light)
9 strips 3" wide (longest needs to be 17") from a variety of browns for the mountain (⅜ yard total)*
¼ yard copper for border spikes
¾ yard green for border background
¼ yard binding
¾ yard backing
26" x 26" batting

* Cut a couple of the pieces in white for a snow-topped mountain.

Foundations

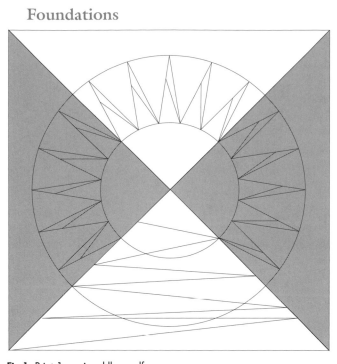

Fig.1. Print 1 sunrise_blk_a.pdf

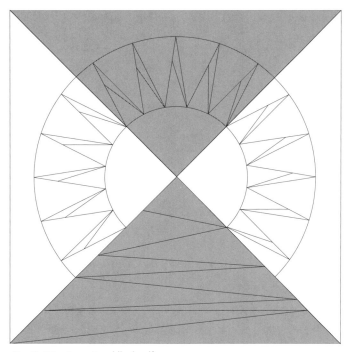

Fig. 2. Print 1 sunrise_blk_b.pdf

Cutting

Cut the outside arcs from the background fabric using templates E, F, and G prior to cutting the spike background pieces. Starch the yardage for ease of handling during the quilt top assembly. Then cut the spikes.

PLACEMENT	COLOR	PIECES NEEDED	SIZE OF EACH PIECE
spikes	medium	15	2" x 4"
spike tips	dark	15	1½" x 5"
spike background	light	18	3½" x 5"
mountain	browns*	9	3" x 17"*

* This is the largest. The pieces get progressively smaller.

Cut 3 sun center arcs using templates H, I, and J.

Sewing Sequence

As with all the quilt projects I do, I always start with the most time consuming part of the quilt and work my way to the easiest. In this case, the sunrise spikey units are the most time-consuming so I started with those. (Actually, the border units are the most time-consuming. But I like to make the quilt top first before I make a final decision on the border.)

Paper piece the sunrise spikey units.

Paper piece the mountain.

Print the border foundations (p. 46).

Assembly

Note: The B and D spikey units are interchangeable. The C unit is a slightly different shape. The same is true of the outer arcs—E and G are interchangeable, F is slightly different. Be careful not to mix them up during the assembly.

Join the sunrise spikes with the center sun arcs (B to H, C to I, and D to J).

Join each unit with its outer arc as shown in figure 3.

Join the units as shown. Trim to measure 16 ⅜" square.

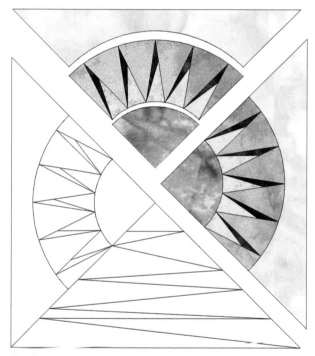

Fig. 3.

Border Foundations

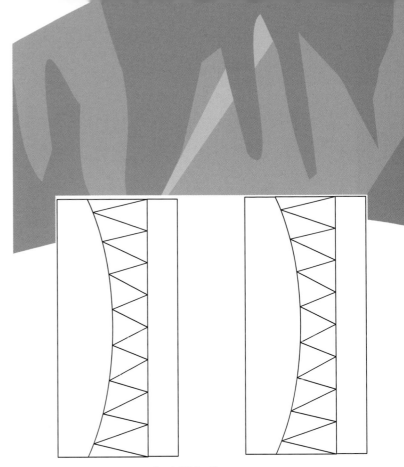

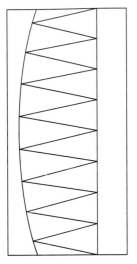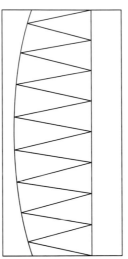

Fig. 4. Print 2 sunrise_bord_blk1.pdf

Fig. 5. Print 4 sunrise_bord_blk2.pdf

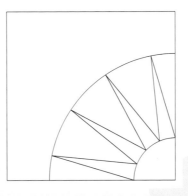

Fig. 6. Print 2 sunrise_corner_blk.pdf

Cutting Chart for Border Blocks and Sunrise Corners

PLACEMENT	COLOR	PIECES NEEDED	SIZE OF EACH PIECE
border block 1 background	green	72	$1\frac{1}{2}"$ x $2\frac{1}{2}"$
border block 1 spikes	copper	64	$1\frac{1}{2}"$ x $2\frac{1}{2}"$
border block 2 background	green	36	$1\frac{1}{2}"$ x $2"$
border block 2 spikes	copper	32	$1\frac{1}{2}"$ x $2"$
border corner background A/C	green	8	scraps
border corner spikes	copper	16	scraps
border corner spikes	green	20	scraps

Paper piece the 12 spikey border units (6 of each) and add the border backgrounds. Do not remove the paper.

Paper piece the Sunrise 4 corner blocks. For border corners that match the quilt on page 43, print one forest_corner.pdf (page 41) and reduce it to 83% on a copy machine. Cut 4 gold A2 spikes and 16 green background pieces for the 4 corner units.

Cut the border backgrounds using the A and B templates for border blocks 1 & 2.

Piece the border spikey units. Join with the matching background pieces.

Join the border units and add to the quilt top as shown (fig. 7).

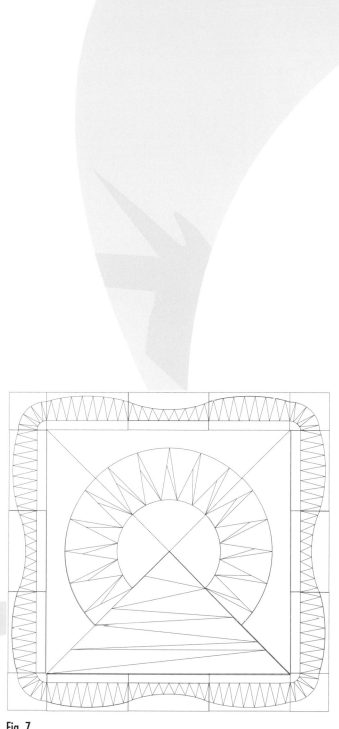

Fig. 7.

Quilting

Quilting was done with a simple meander in matching thread. The border pieces are outline quilted to enhance their spikiness.

CHAPTER 4
A BREAK FROM TRADITION

I have always been drawn to the traditional New York Beauty block. Its striking simplicity always pulls me in, but I always feel there is a little something missing.

When I started making the RINGO STAR quilt, the traditional New York Beauty block was a factor that led to that design. However, when I started HOMMAGE À LA BEAUTÉ DE NEW YORK, I knew I was getting what I really hoped for—a New York Beauty with attitude!

I even found myself working on it at a slower pace, relishing each and every spike. As it took shape, I smiled a lot. I really thought I had finally given the traditional quilt a fresh, new face. I hope you all agree!

At the same time as this quilt was being made, I learned of my twin nieces' battle against cancer. RIBBONS OF HOPE just came to me and I simply *had* to make it as well. I still haven't figured out which traditional pattern it reminds me of, but surely there is one out there. If anyone has a clue, let me know!

RINGO STAR

44" x 44", made by author

This
is a
delightful
little quilt
that will help
you hone your
paper-piecing
skills as well as
clear out some of
those little bitlets of
fabric you have lying
around your sewing room.

Although this was designed
as a baby quilt, it's been made in
a variety of renditions and used for
table toppers and wallhangings. Use
your imagination and make what works for
you!

There are only two basic blocks, so it goes
together pretty quickly. Enjoy the fun of making
your own color and fabric choices. Dig through
that stash and see what you can come up with!

Yardage

Scraps for inner block spikes and Flying Geese (¼ yard total)

1¾ yards for inner block background and block arcs

12 assorted 2" x 27" strips for outer block spikes

12 assorted 3" x 28" strips for outer block spike background

½ yard inner and outer borders

¼ yard middle border

⅜ yard binding

3⅛ yard backing

52" x 52" batting

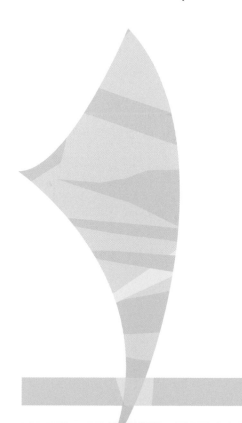

Foundations

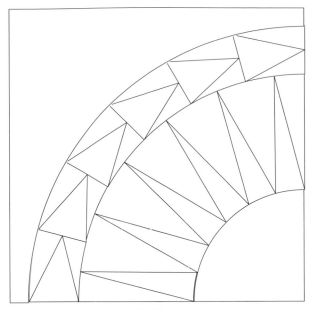

Fig. 1. Print 4 ringo_center_blk.pdf

Cutting

Center Blocks Cutting Chart

PLACEMENT	FABRIC	PIECES NEEDED	SIZE OF EACH PIECE
center block spikes	assorted	24	2" x 4$\frac{1}{2}$"
center block spike background	light	28	1$\frac{1}{2}$" x 5"
Flying Geese	assorted	24	2$\frac{1}{2}$" x 2$\frac{1}{2}$"
center block Flying Geese background	light	48	1$\frac{1}{2}$" x 3"
arcs	light	4	9" x 9"

Starch the 9" squares and cut 4 pairs of inside and outside arcs using templates A and B.

Cut the pieces for the 12 outer blocks.

Outer Blocks Cutting Chart

PLACEMENT	FABRIC	PIECES NEEDED	SIZE OF EACH PIECE
outer block spikes	assorted	72 (6 from each strip)	2" x 4$\frac{1}{2}$"
outer block spike background	assorted	84 (7 from each strip)	1$\frac{1}{2}$" x 5"
block arcs	light	12	9" x 9"

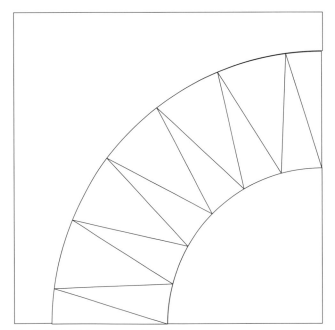

Fig. 2. Print 12 ringo_outer_blk.pdf

Starch the 9" squares and cut 12 pairs of inside and outside arcs using templates B and C.

Sewing Sequence

Piece the 4 inner block spikey units (fig. 3).

Ease on the inside arcs. Remember, this is not a race. Going a bit slower for curves is not only OK, it's required. It takes a lot of practice to whip them into place with speed, so for now, let's take our time. Press and set aside.

Follow the numbering to piece the Flying Geese units.

Ease on the outside arcs and remove the paper from the geese.

Ease the geese units onto the spikey units. Remove the paper, press, and square up the blocks.

Piece the 12 outer block spikey units (fig. 4).

Ease on the inside and outside arcs. Remove the paper, press, and square up the blocks.

Fig. 4.

Fig. 3.

Join the blocks as shown (fig. 5).

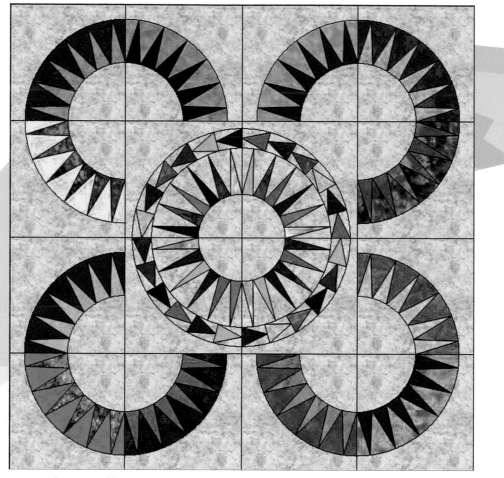

Fig. 5. Quilt top assembly

Border

Cut 9 strips 2" wide for the inner and outer borders.

Cut 4 strips 1¼" wide for the middle border.

Add to the quilt as shown in the photo on page 50, piecing the outside border as necessary.

Quilting

Have fun with the quilting.

Because I made this as a baby quilt, I felt the quilting should be somewhat dense so it would stand up to repeated washings. Refer to the detail in the quilt photo. Of course most people try and hang my quilts but I like the kids to use them.

HOMMAGE À LA BEAUTÉ DE NEW YORK

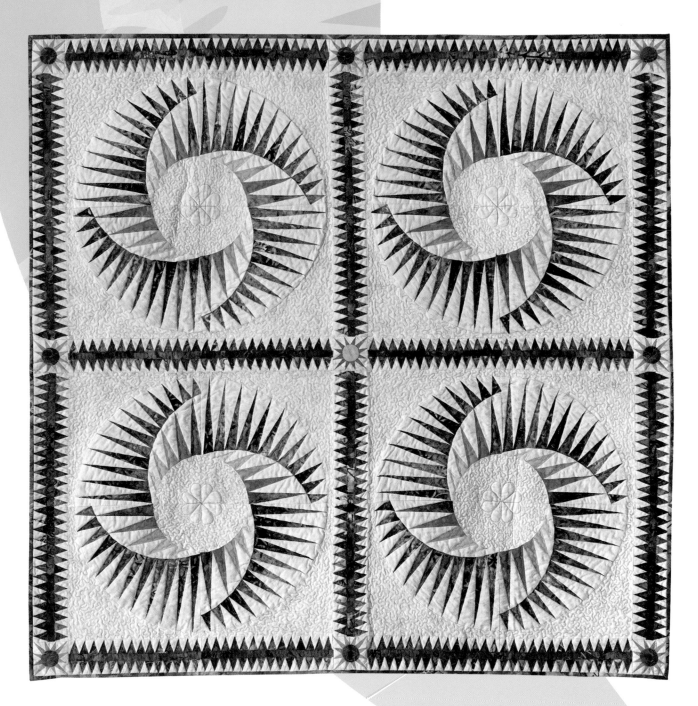

44" x 44", made by author

While working on the various projects in this book, it occurred to me that I'd never done a classic New York Beauty quilt. A very strange feeling swept over me as I realized the New York Beauty was my inspiration for creating all the quilts I make. I owed it to this block to create something, well, *almost* like the classic pattern.

The double-arc blocks are easier than they look and they went together in an afternoon, but I can't say the same for the sashing blocks. Let's just say I now have far greater appreciation for all those women from years past who made sashing and borders like these. Making them using a paper-piecing method certainly is faster than in yesteryear but still time-consuming. I can't imagine doing them by hand but I will admit the work was well worth it. I now have my very own almost classic New York Beauty quilt.

So, now that you're ready to get going on your very own "homage" quilt, let's get started!

I used a delicious selection of Timeless Treasures batiks. I know, I know. A true homage would use standard cotton prints in two colors, but I'm a bit of a rebel and used one color for the background and six different batiks for the spikes and sashings. Of course, if you're more of a purist, by all means use just two colors!

There are 16 blocks in this quilt and I've figured everything based on that number. If you want to make this quilt larger or smaller, divide my numbers by 16 to get the figures you need for each block. Then you can multiply by the number of blocks you want to make.

Each 10" block will look like this when sewn (fig. 1).

Fig. 1.

Yardage

7 yards background fabric (shown in ivory)

4 yards for spikes in outer arcs, sashing, and borders

5 fat quarters, 1 in each of 5 colors, for the inner arc spikes

³⁄₈ yard binding

3 yards backing

52" x 52" batting

Foundations

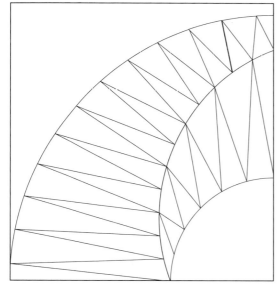

Fig. 2. Print 16 hommage_block.pdf

Cutting

Starch 1¼ yards of background fabric and cut out 16 squares 11" x 11". Cut 16 inside and outside arcs using templates C and D.

We'll do the rest of the cutting as we go along to help keep things straight.

Sewing Sequence

I know that some folks want to skip the cutting of the smaller pieces, but believe me, it's a lot less wasteful of fabric and far quicker to piece this way. The extra time it takes to make the stacks saves you twice as much time as you would spend trying to piece with the fabrics still in long strips.

Outer Spikey Arcs

Cut 24 strips 1½" wide across the width of your outer arc spike yardage.

Cut 16 pieces of each size and place in stacks arranged in the order they'll be sewn, starting with the smallest spike pieces.

1½" x 7"

1½" x 6½"

1½" x 6¼"

1½" x 6"

1½" x 5¼"

1½" x 4¾"

1½" x 4½"

1½" x 4¼"

1½" x 4"

1½" x 3½"

1½" x 3¼"

1½" x 3"

Cut 24 strips 2" wide across the width of your background fabric.

Cut 16 pieces of each size and place in stacks arranged in the order they'll be sewn, starting with the smallest background pieces.

2" x 7½"

2" x 7"

2" x 6½"

2" x 6¼"

2" x 6"

2" x 5¼"

2" x 4¾"

2" x 4½"

2" x 4¼"

2" x 4"

2" x 3½"

2" x 3¼"

2" x 3"

2³/₄" x 3"
2³/₄" x 3¹/₂"
2³/₄" x 4¹/₂"
2³/₄" x 5¹/₂"
2³/₄" x 6¹/₂"
2³/₄" x 7"

Piece the inner spikey arc units. Do not remove the paper.

Gently ease the inside arcs (C) onto the inner spikey units. Now you can remove the paper from the inner spikey unit. Press the seam allowance toward the inside arc.

Ease the inner spikey arc unit onto the outer spikey arc unit. NOW you can remove any remaining paper and press open. Pretty spiffy, huh? And you thought this was going to be difficult, didn't you?

OK, let's finish all those blocks up, slap them up on the design wall in groups of 4 as shown, and admire your work (fig. 3). (This part feels so good, doesn't it?)

Remember, when starting the first piece, the back of the background fabric is the first thing to touch the back of the foundation paper.

Piece the outer spikey arc units. Do not remove the paper.

Gently ease the outside arcs (D) onto the outer spikey units. Do not remove the paper yet.

Inner Spikey Arcs

I used a gradation of yellow-to-orange batiks on the inner spikey arcs. For cutting purposes, I will refer to the colors I used.

Cut 2" wide strips perpendicular to the fat quarter selvage. Cut 16 pieces of each color and place in stacks.

COLOR	STRIPS	CUT INTO 16 PIECES
light yellow	3	2" x 3"
dark yellow	3	2" x 3¹/₂"
light orange	4	2" x 4¹/₂"
medium orange	4	2" x 5¹/₂"
darkest orange	6	2" x 6¹/₂"

Cut 12 strips 2³/₄" wide across the width of the background fabric. Cut 16 pieces of each size and place in stacks arranged in the order they'll be sewn, starting with the longest background pieces.

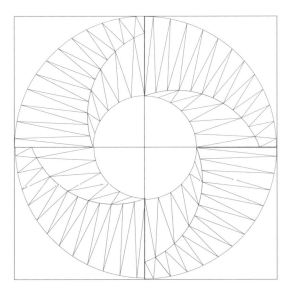

Fig. 3. Block placement diagram

Sashing and Borders

Now that you're feeling all warm and fuzzy inside with that sense of accomplishment swirling around you, it's time to start cutting for the sashing and borders.

These units are very time consuming, but don't get discouraged. Trust me, it's worth the effort to finish these.

My sashing and border fabrics are the same ones I used for the outer arcs. It's a scrumptious Timeless Treasures batik that has, without a doubt, the most amazing colors all swirling around in it. As you cut it, you get different little bitlets of color showing up here and there. In my opinion, it gives the quilt a lot more life.

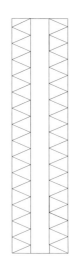

Fig. 4. Print 24 hommage_sashing.pdf

Each border/sashing block unit has two spikey strips with a plain strip in the middle. Check the foundation length against your finished blocks and trim if necessary before piecing.

Cutting for the Border

Cut 34 strips 1½" wide across the width of the spike fabric.

Cut into 672 pieces 1½" x 2".

Cut 8 strips 1" wide across the width of the spike fabric.

Cut into 24 pieces for the middle strip.

Cut 36 strips 1½" wide across the width of the background fabric.

Cut into 720 pieces ½" x 2".

Paper piece 24 sashing/border blocks. Do not remove the paper yet.

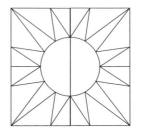

Fig. 5. Print 9 hommage_cornerstn.pdf

I admit it, I cheated here. This is a very small block and even I shuddered at the thought of piecing those tiny little inner arcs, so I appliquéd a circle over the finished spikey units. Piece or appliqué the centers, whichever way you prefer.

I used the same orange fabrics I used in the inner spikey unit of the basic blocks as I had a lot of scraps left from piecing them. (Waste not, want not; that's my motto.) If you're not using scraps, cut the pieces as follows:

Cut 12 strips 1" wide from spike fabrics perpendicular to the fat quarter selvage. Cut into 108 pieces 1" x 2".

Cut 8 strips 1½" wide across the width of the background fabric. Cut into 144 pieces 1½" x 2".

If you're going to paper piece the center, cut out 18 half-centers using the B and D templates (9 each).

If you decide to appliqué a center circle instead, you can use a half-dollar piece as a template. It works perfectly. Trace and cut out 9 circles, adding a ¼" seam allowance.

Paper piece the spikey units. Ease in the arcs (B & D) and join the 2 halves to complete the cornerstone blocks OR join the halves first and appliqué the center circle in place.

Quilt Assembly

Join sets of 4 blocks, sashing units, and cornerstones as shown (fig. 6).

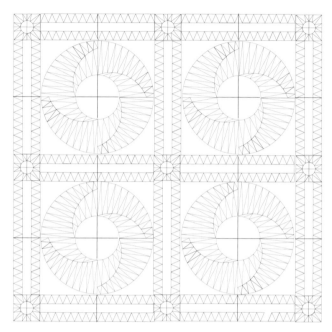

Fig. 6. Quilt top assembly

Wasn't all that piecing worth it? Come on, admit it, it was!

Quilting

Quilting is a very personal finishing touch, but here's what I did for this one.

RIBBONS OF HOPE

43" x 43", made by author

We
all have stories
about friends, sisters,
mothers, daughters, and even
strangers with cancer. I don't think that
my story is any different from anyone else's,
but I found myself at a juncture in my life that I
HAD to make this quilt.

I have beautiful twin nieces (who will probably smack me when they see I've written about them in this book) who had a profound impact on the design of this quilt. Their mother died of breast cancer at the age of 40. That, in and of itself, was beyond tragic for two young children, but when faced with the same danger themselves in adulthood, they made the most extraordinary decision to fight for their lives.

At 34 years of age, they decided to undergo radical mastectomies and ovary removal in order to preempt what they felt (and medical science agreed) was the inevitable battle with cancer. This decision was not an easy one, but with the support of their families and friends, these two beautiful women proceeded with courage and dignity.

During this time, this quilt came to me in a dream. It looked far easier in my head than it was when I tried to design it. But fear not—it's not a difficult quilt, just a bit more time consuming. I think the results are well worth it.

As
you can
see I chose
pinks. For those of
you who know me, I
NEVER gravitate toward
pink but it just seemed right.
I didn't give in to cutesy fabrics
but chose all batiks. Who knew there
were so many incredibly luscious pink
batiks?

Yardage

I used five different pinks in the quilt from light to dark.

¼ yard pink #1 light pink
⅓ yard pink #2 medium pink
¼ yard pink #3 dark pink
⅓ yard pink #4 darker pink
¼ yard pink # 5 darkest pink

½ yard multicolored batik (for inner arc spikes)
½ yard green
2 yards light background
1¼ yards dark border background
⅜ yard binding
3 yards backing
51" x 51" batting

Foundations

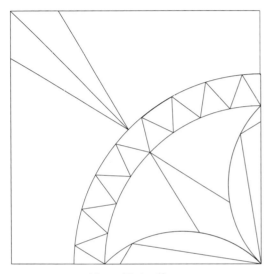

Fig. 1. print 16 ribbons_block.pdf

Cutting

PLACEMENT	COLOR	PIECES NEEDED	SIZE OF EACH PIECE
C1	darker pink	16	3½" x 6"
A3 & B3	medium pink	32	1½" x 6"
A2 & B2	darkest pink	32	1½" x 2"
E1	dark pink	16	2½" x 6"
E2	light pink	16	2½" x 6"
D spikes	multi	128	2" x 2"
D background	green	144	2" x 2"
A1 & B1	light background	32	2" x 6"
C2 & C3	light background	32	5" x 5"
E3 & E4	light background	32	5" x 8"

Cut the pieces for the 16 blocks. Placement is indicated with the foundation labels.

You'll have enough of the pinks left over for the border blocks. We'll cut the rest of the pieces as we go along to help keep things straight.

Sewing Sequence

I've labeled the block to show which pink is which (fig. 2). This block is a series of curves, but easy curves to sew. Trust me!

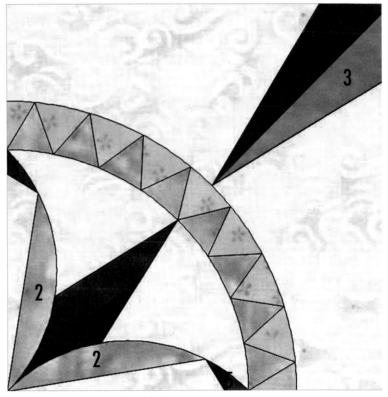

Fig. 2. RIBBONS OF HOPE block

Start with the side curved sections (A and B) and paper piece 16 of each section in the sequence indicated on the foundation.

Piece 16 center curved sections (C). Starch and press these, then remove the paper.

Gently ease the A and B units onto the C unit. I didn't need pins for this as it's such a graceful curve, but do what feels best for you. Try with and without pinning and go with the

method that's easiest for you. Remember, this is NOT a race. Take your time with these blocks and they will come out perfectly.

Paper piece the outer arc of spikes (D). Leave the paper on and join with the A/B/C unit.

Paper piece the large outer spike arc (E). Ease onto the A/B/C/D units. Remove all the paper and press.

Arrange the blocks into rows as shown. Join the blocks into rows, then sew the rows together (fig. 3).

Fig. 3. Quilt top assembly

Border

I opted for a simple outer border. It's quite pleasing and gives the center of the quilt a chance to shine, don't you think?

Foundations

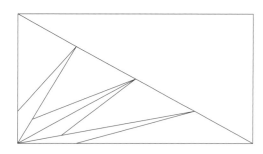

Fig. 4. Print 4 ribbons_border_a.pdf

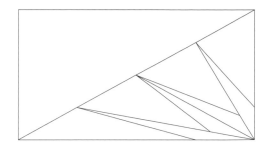

Fig. 5. Print 4ribbons_border_b.pdf

Cut the pieces for the border blocks. Placement is indicated with the foundation labels.

Border Blocks A and B

PLACEMENT	COLOR	PIECES NEEDED	SIZE OF EACH PIECE
A1	medium pink	8	$1\frac{1}{2}$" x 6"
A2 & A5	light pink	16	$1\frac{1}{2}$" x 6"
A3 & A4	background	16	$3\frac{1}{2}$" x 5"
A6	dark pink	8	$1\frac{1}{2}$" x 8"
A7 & A8	background	16	$2\frac{1}{2}$" x 8"
A9	background	8	5" x 11"

Paper piece the border blocks (A and B) and join in pairs. (Refer to quilt photo on page 62.)

Cut 3 strips 5" wide of background fabric for the outer border.

Cut 4 pieces 5" x 12" and sew to the ends of paired border blocks. Add to the top and bottom of the quilt, centering the border blocks, and trim to the width of the quilt.

Cut 4 pieces 5" x 17" and sew to the ends of the 2 remaining paired border blocks. Add to the sides of the quilt, centering the border blocks, and trim as before.

Quilting

I struggled with quilting motifs for weeks. Nothing seemed quite right, but I settled on this. I think the patterns I chose work well with the quilt. What do you think?

CHAPTER 5

ATTITUDES EMERGE

Now that I was liberated by making my New York Beauty quilt, I had some wilder patterns floating around in my head, fighting to get out. I've learned never to argue with them—just design them and start sewing.

So the quilts in this chapter are those quilts that won!

ARIZONA SUNRISE is not exactly wild, but it is a break from the traditional for sure. Depending on the color choices you make, it could indeed become a psychedelic tapestry of your fabrics!

CROWN OF ISIS and FIREWORKS are definitely outside the box. DREAM CATCHER is one of my calmer quilts, or at least I see it that way, but I'll let you decide. I hope you enjoy them all.

ARIZONA SUNRISE

47" x 47", made by author

There are several renditions of this quilt floating around out there and I never seem to tire of making new ones. With just a simple change of color or pattern here and there, she takes on an entirely different look. So, depending on how you want to play with color, I'll list requirements based on the colors in this quilt. I encourage you to change any or all of them to create your own masterpiece!

Yardage

Yardage is given for the colors I used. Feel free to substitute your own!

¼ yard purple for inner block spikes

⅜ yard gold for inner block spike background and outer block spikes

1¾ yard orange for inner block spikes, inner block arcs, and outer block spike background

½ yard dark blue for inner block arcs

1⅞ yards turquoise for inner block spike background, outer block arcs, inner border, outer border spike background, and corners

2½ yards ivory for background and outer block arcs

⅜ yard binding

3 ¼ yards backing

55" x 55" batting

Foundations

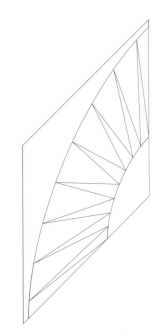

Fig. 2. Print 8 az_sun_outer_blk.pdf

Cutting

We'll cut as we go along to help keep things straight.

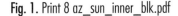

Fig. 1. Print 8 az_sun_inner_blk.pdf

Sewing Sequence

Cut the pieces for the inner spikey blocks.

PLACEMENT	COLOR	PIECES NEEDED	SIZE OF EACH PIECE
inner arc spikes	purple	56	$2\frac{3}{4}$" x $4\frac{1}{2}$"
inner arc background	gold	64	2" x $4\frac{1}{2}$"
outer arc spikes	orange	56	$1\frac{1}{2}$" x $2\frac{1}{2}$"
outer arc background	turquoise	64	$1\frac{1}{2}$" x $2\frac{1}{2}$"

Starch the orange and dark blue yardage and cut 8 inside arcs (B) from the orange fabric and 8 outside arcs (D) from the dark blue fabric.

Stack the purple and gold pieces. *Remember, when you start piecing each unit, the back of the background fabric is the first thing to touch the back of the paper.*

Paper piece the inner spikey arcs (A). Trim on the outside cutting line and set aside. Do not remove the paper yet.

Stack the orange and turquoise pieces. Paper piece the outer spikey arcs (C). Trim on the outside cutting line and set aside. Do not remove the paper yet.

Sew units A and B together, easing the inside arc (B) onto the spikey unit (A).

Sew units C and D together, easing the outside arc (D) onto the spikey unit (C).

Remove the paper from the outer spikey unit and sew the two spikey units together. Remove the remaining paper.

Cut the pieces for the outer spikey blocks.

PLACEMENT	COLOR	PIECES NEEDED	SIZE OF EACH PIECE
spikes	gold	64	$1\frac{1}{2}$" x $5\frac{3}{4}$"
spike background	orange	72	$2\frac{1}{2}$" x $5\frac{1}{2}$"

Starch the turquoise and ivory background yardage and cut 8 inside arcs (B) from the turquoise fabric and 8 outside arcs (C) from the ivory fabric.

Paper piece the spikey unit (A).

Ease the inside (B) and outside (C) arcs onto the spikey units. Remove the paper.

Quilt Top Assembly

Cut 8 squares of background fabric $8\frac{3}{4}$" x $8\frac{3}{4}$".

Cut 2 squares of background fabric 13" x 13" in half on the diagonal.

Join the inner blocks, leaving $\frac{1}{4}$" of the seam open at the outer edge. Sew 4 pairs of blocks, then join the pairs into 2 sets of 4 blocks, and sew the final seam to join all 8 blocks. Press the seam allowances toward the center.

Set in the ring of $8\frac{3}{4}$" squares using traditional Y-seam piecing. Start $\frac{1}{4}$" in from the outside edge, stitch to the Y intersection, pivot, and stitch out to the opposite edge, stopping $\frac{1}{4}$" from the end.

Set in the 8 spikey outer blocks in the same way.

Add the triangles to the four corners to complete the top.

Cut 5 turquoise strips 1½" wide for the inner border.

Piece the border units. Join them into 4 strips of 3 units each. Remove the paper. Add cornerstones to the ends of two of the strips.

Add the borders as shown (fig. 6).

Fig. 3. Quilt top assembly

Border Foundations

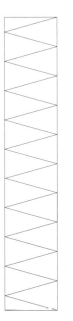

Fig. 5. Print 4 az_sun_corner.pdf

Fig. 6. ARIZONA SUN border assembly

Fig. 4. Print 12 az_sun_border.pdf

Cut the pieces for the border.

PLACEMENT	COLOR	PIECES NEEDED	SIZE OF EACH PIECE
spikes	orange	120	2½" x 3½"
spike background	turquoise	132	2½" x 3½"
corner spike	orange	4	2" x 5"
corner background	turquoise	8	2½" x 4½"

Quilting

Quilt as desired! This is what I did.

Deb Kara

CROWN OF ISIS

60" x 60", made by author

While
I was making this
quilt, I must have had a
hundred names in my head for it.
For a month or so, I referred to this quilt as
EGYPT, but it never quite fit. CROWN OF ISIS came
to me in a dream and when I looked up who Isis
was (besides knowing she was somehow attached
to Egyptian mythology) I knew the name was
perfect.

Isis was the goddess of magic and healing.
I have always believed that quilts contain the
magic of their creators. Babies sleep better under
handmade quilts than store bought; hospital
patients find a calm after the storm of disease
while sleeping under handmade quilts. No one
can convince me they don't contain magic. So
the name apparently was given to me as a symbol
of this meaning.

I hope you like it enough to try and make
one for yourself, allowing your own creative
juices to make it up in your favorite color
combos.

As with all the other quilts, I'll give you the
yardage requirements according to the colors
I used, and you can just drop your own in and
color it according to your preferences.

The center blocks are colored to show a
slight glow in the center of each one. There are
four yellow/oranges in each one, starting
with the lightest in the center and working
outwards to the darker ones. I've numbered them, because
they're repeated throughout the quilt, and it will help when you go to
purchase or pull from your stash.

Yardage

⅛ yard light red (1)
¼ yard red (2)
⅛ yard darker red (3)
⅜ yard light yellow (1)
1⅞ yards yellow (2)
⅝ yard darker yellow (3)
⅜ yard darkest yellow (4)
⅜ yard lightest blue (1)
⅜ yard light blue (2)
1 yard blue (3)
⅜ yard dark blue (4)
½ yard darker blue (5)

⅜ yard very darkest blue (6)
4¼ yards background
½ yard binding
4 yards backing
70" x 70" batting

Foundations

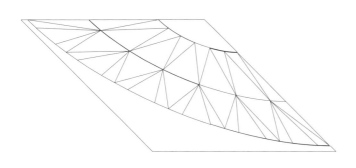

Fig. 1. Print 8 crown_center_blk

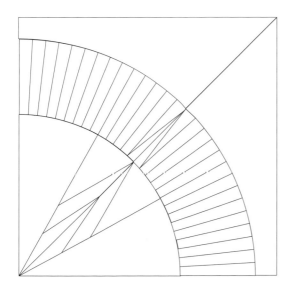

Fig. 2. Print 8 crown_middle_blk

Fig. 3. Print 8 crown_outer_blk

Cutting

As with the other more complex designs, we'll cut as we go along.

Sewing Sequence

Let's start with the center blocks.

Cutting Chart for Center Blocks

Label the pieces as you cut them, then stack them in sewing (numerical) sequence.

PLACEMENT	COLOR	PIECES NEEDED	SIZE OF EACH PIECE
INNER ARC A (SPIKES)			
A6, A8	(1) light red (at center)	16	1½" x 3½
A4, A10	(2) red	16	1½" x 4"
A2, A12	(3) darker red	16	1½" x 4½"
INNER ARC A (BACKGROUND)			
A7	(1) light yellow	8	3½" x 3½"
A5, A9	(2) yellow	16	3½" x 4"
A3, A11	(3) darker yellow	16	2½" x4½"
A1, A13	(4) darkest yellow	16	1½" x 5"
OUTER ARC B (SPIKES)			
B12, B14	(1) light yellow	16	1½" x 3½
B8, B10, B16, B18	(2) yellow	32	1½" x 4½"
B4, B6, B20, B22	(3) darker yellow	32	1½" x 4½"
B2, B24	(4) darkest yellow	16	1½" x 5½"
OUTER ARC B (BACKGROUND)			
B11, B13, B15	(1) lightest blue	24	3" x 3½"
B9, B17	(2) light blue	16	2½" x 3½"
B7, B19	(3) blue	16	2½" x 3 ½"
B5, B21	(4) dark blue	16	2½" x 4 1/2"
B3, B23	(5) darker blue	16	2" x 5"
B1, B25	(6) very darkest blue	16	1½" x 5"

Starch yellow #3 and cut out 8 inside arcs using the D template.

Starch the background fabric and cut out 8 outside arcs using the C template.

Remember, *the back of the background fabric is the first thing to touch the back of the paper foundation.* You will start sewing between numbers one and two on the foundation pattern.

Paper piece the A spikey arcs.

Gently ease on the inside arc (D) piece.

As you finish each unit pin it up on your design wall but do not remove any paper yet. Aren't they scrumptious? I just adore watching my quilts come to life on my design wall; it's like a kind of childbirth for me every time. This is the most exciting part of quilting for me. I watch those little bitlets of fabric forming into a beautiful quilt. There are just no words to describe this process.

Paper piece the B spikey arcs.

Gently ease on the outside arc (C) piece.

Remove the paper from the B spikey arcs.

With the paper side down, right sides together, ease the B spikey arcs onto the A spikey arcs.

Remove all the remaining paper. Press the blocks and put them back up on your design wall.

Let's stick with the same colors and do the outermost blocks next. These blocks are constructed in halves, then joined during the quilt assembly to avoid Y-seam construction.

Cutting Chart for Outer Ring Blocks

Label the pieces as you cut them, then stack them in sewing (numerical) sequence.

PLACEMENT	COLOR	PIECES NEEDED	SIZE OF EACH PIECE
INNER ARC **A & B**			
A & B even	red (2)	48	$1\frac{1}{2}"$ x $2"$
A & B odd	darker yellow (3)	48	$1\frac{1}{2}"$ x $2"$
OUTER ARC **C & D** (SPIKES)			
C12, D2	light yellow (1)	16	$1\frac{1}{2}"$ x $3\frac{1}{2}"$
C 8, C10, D4, D6	yellow (2)	32	$1\frac{1}{2}"$ x $4\frac{1}{2}"$
C4, C6, D8, D10	darker yellow (3)	32	$1\frac{1}{2}"$ x $4\frac{1}{2}"$
C2, D12	darkest yellow (4)	16	$1\frac{1}{2}"$ x $5\frac{1}{2}"$
OUTER ARC **C & D** (BACKGROUND)			
C11, C13, D1, D3	lightest blue (1)	32	$3"$ x $3\frac{1}{2}"$
C9, D5	light blue (2)	16	$2\frac{1}{2}"$ x $3\frac{1}{2}"$
C7, D7	blue (3)	16	$2\frac{1}{2}"$ x $3\frac{1}{2}"$
C5, D9	dark blue (4)	16	$2\frac{1}{2}"$ x $4\frac{1}{2}"$
C3, D11	darker blue (5)	16	$2"$ x $5"$
C1, D13	very darkest blue (6)	16	$1\frac{1}{2}"$ x $5"$

Starch the background (darkest blue) fabric and cut 16 inside arcs (E and G) and 16 outside arcs (F and H).

Paper piece the inner spikey arcs (A and B).
Join with the inside arcs (A with E and B with G). Do not remove the paper.
Paper piece the outer spikey arcs (C and D).
Join with the outside arcs (C with F and D with H).
Remove the paper from the outer spikey arcs.
Join the outer and inner arc units.
Remove all the remaining paper.
Press and place the blocks on the design wall.

Finally, let's do the middle square blocks, which are also constructed in halves. You'll be surprised at how many scraps you can use up from the inner and outer blocks on these.

Cutting Chart for the Middle Blocks

PLACEMENT	COLOR	PIECES NEEDED	Size
INNER SPIKEY ARCS B & E			
C1, D1	lightest blue (1)	16	$1\frac{1}{2}"$ x $5\frac{1}{2}"$
C2, D2	yellow (2)	16	$1\frac{1}{2}"$ x 6"
C3, D3	background	16	$1\frac{1}{2}"$ x 4"
C4, D4	background	16	4" x $7\frac{1}{2}"$
MIDDLE SPIKEY ARCS A & B (SPIKES)			
A15, B1	yellow (2)	16	$1\frac{1}{2}"$ x 6"
A13, B3	lightest blue (1)	16	$1\frac{1}{2}"$ x 4"
A11, B5	light blue (2)	16	$1\frac{1}{2}"$ x 4"
A9, B7	blue (3)	16	$1\frac{1}{2}"$ x 4"
A7, B9	dark blue (4)	16	$1\frac{1}{2}"$ x 4"
A5, B11	darker blue (5)	16	1" x 4"
A3, A1, B13, B15	very darkest blue (6)	32	$1\frac{1}{2}"$ x 4"
MIDDLE SPIKEY ARCS A & B (BACKGROUND)			
A & B even	yellow (2)	112	$1\frac{1}{2}"$ x 4"

Starch the background fabric and cut 8 each E and F outside arcs.

Paper piece the inner spikey arcs (C & D). Remove the paper.

Paper piece the middle spikey arcs (A & B).

Join the middle spikey arcs with the outside arcs (A to E and B to F).

Add to the inner spikey arcs (A/E to C and B/F to D)

Remove all the remaining paper.

Press and place the blocks on the design wall. Do not joint the halves.

At this point, the WOW factor starts happening! I generally stand back at this point and marvel at the new quilt forming. Is it all you wanted it to be? Would you rearrange the blocks or keep them just as I've designed them? There are NO quilt police, so feel free to have fun with these blocks. You can change them, rotate them, anything. Now's the time.

Quilt Top Assembly

The quilt top is constructed in kite-shaped wedges. Each wedge is a mirror image of its adjoining wedge. The half-blocks eliminate any extreme Y-seams (fig. 4.)

Join the wedges as shown.

Fig. 4. Wedge assembly

Arrange the wedges and join as shown (fig. 5).

Fig. 5. Quilt top assembly

Cut 2 squares of background fabric 16" x 16" in half on the diagonal.

Sew onto the corners as shown. Trim away the excess as you square up the quilt top.

Isn't it lovely? Now you have the option of adding a border like I did, creating your own, or simply stopping here. It's up to you. This is your quilt.

Borders

If you choose to do my border, again, I used the yellows and blues that I used in the main quilt, with the exception that I only used one blue and one yellow.

Foundations

Fig. 6. Print 4 crown_border_a.pdf

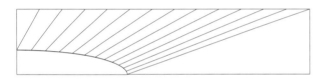

Fig. 7. Print 4 crown_border_a.pdf

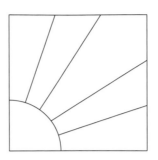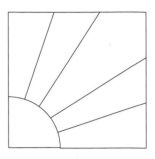

Fig. 8. Print 2 crown_corner_blk.pdf

Cutting Chart for Border Blocks

PLACEMENT	COLOR	PIECES NEEDED	SIZE OF EACH PIECE
OUTER ARC SPIKES			
A even	yellow (2)	48	2" x 10"*
A odd	blue (3)	56	2" x 10"*
A 14	background	8	10" x 4"
CORNER SPIKES			
A odd	yellow (3)	12	2¼" x 4"
A even	blue (2)	8	2¼" x 4"

*Note: This is the size for the longest pieces. They get progressively shorter, so you may need only half the number indicated.

Starch the yellow fabric and cut out 8 border block inside arcs (B) and 4 corner inside arcs (B).

Cut 4 strips 3½" wide from background fabric to join with the border blocks.

Cut 7 strips 3" wide from background fabric for the final outer border.

Paper piece the spikey arc units.

Ease on the inside arcs.

Align two border blocks with the edges of one side of the quilt top. Measure the distance between the two blocks. Add ½" and cut a strip that length from a 3½" border strip. Sew a border block to each end and add to the side of the quilt top. Repeat on the other side. (Refer to the quilt photo on page 73.)

Join the corner units to the remaining border blocks and in the same way, cut and add a border strip and join to the sides of the quilt.

Quilting

I could just say "quilt as desired," but this seems to be one of the hardest hurdles for some to handle, so I like to give a little guidance. I've shown close-ups of my quilting and hope you'll find some inspiration there!

FIREWORKS

62" x 62", made by author

Designs don't always start with a pattern that I then fill in with fabric. In some cases, I start with chunks of fabric that please me and build a design from there. This is one of those quilts.

Do you have some fabrics in your stash that you just don't know what to do with? Are there those precious ones that you fear cutting into? Well, this quilt is the product of my stash favorites.

I stood by my stash (which is a closet filled with fabrics) and was drawn to some reds and oranges. I adore these fabrics but just couldn't figure out what I wanted to do with them. I hung a bunch of them up on my design wall and stared aimlessly at them for almost a week. Then I saw a fireworks show on TV (You don't think I'm actually going to sit outside here in San Francisco and watch fireworks do you?) and it came to me—exploding fireworks!

Out came the laptop and I started playing with designs. The beauty of this design is that you can make it scrappy or make it with carefully controlled colors. Either way, it will still look stunning!

Look closely at center blocks 1 and 2. The diagonal and square settings are what make the difference. They're both the exact same design.

Yardage

⅜ yard light blue
⅜ yard medium blue
6½ yards blue-black background and outer border

⅜ yard each of a gradation from light to dark:
    lightest yellow
    light yellow
    yellow
    pale orange
    orange
    dark orange
    orange-red
    red-orange
¼ yard each lavender, light purple, purple, and dark purple
¼ yard red for inner border and binding
4 yards backing
70" x 70" batting

Foundations

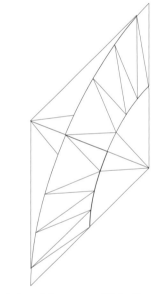

Fig. 1. Print 8 fire_center_blk1.pdf

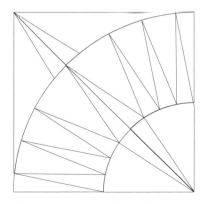

Fig. 2. Print 8 fire_center_blk2.pdf

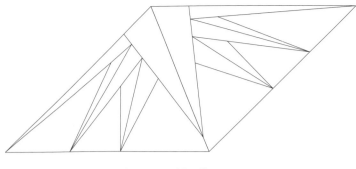

Fig. 3. Print 16 fire_outter_blk.pdf

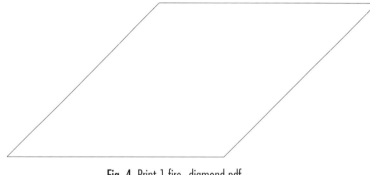

Fig. 4. Print 1 fire_diamond.pdf

SPIKES BACKGROUND			
PLACEMENT	FABRIC	PIECES NEEDED	SIZE OF EACH PIECE
A1	lightest yellow	8	$1^1/2$" x 5"
A3	light yellow	8	$1^1/2$" x $4^1/2$"
A5	yellow	8	2" x 4"
A7	pale orange	8	3" x $3^1/2$"
B2	orange	8	3" x $3^1/2$"
B4	dark orange	8	2" x 4"
B6	orange-red	8	$1^1/2$" x $4^1/2$"
B8	red-orange	8	$1^1/2$" x 5

Shade the background pieces from the lightest yellow (A1) to the dark red-orange (B8).

SPIKES			
PLACEMENT	FABRIC	PIECES NEEDED	SIZE OF EACH PIECE
A2	lavender	8	$1^1/2$" x $4^1/2$"
A4	light purple	8	$1^1/2$" x $4^1/2$"
A6	light purple	8	$1^3/4$" x 4"
A8	medium blue	8	$1^3/4$" x 3"
B1	light blue	8	$1^3/4$" x 3"
B3	purple	8	$1^3/4$" x 4"
B5	purple	8	$1^1/2$" x $4^1/2$"
B7	dark purple	8	$1^1/2$" x $4^1/2$"

OUTER ARC			
PLACEMENT	FABRIC	PIECES NEEDED	SIZE OF EACH PIECE
C1 & D1	blue-black	16	$2^1/2$" x 8"
C2	medium blue	8	2" x $2^1/2$"
D2	light blue	8	2" x $2^1/2$"

Paper piece the inner arcs, the middle spikey units, and the outer arcs.

Don't forget—the back of the background fabric is the first thing to touch the back of the paper.

Remove the paper from the inner arcs and ease them onto the middle spikey units.

Remove the paper from the outer arcs and ease them onto the middle spikey units.

Join the halves.

Cutting

Cutting Charts for Center Block 1

INNER ARC			
PLACEMENT	FABRIC	PIECES NEEDED	SIZE OF EACH PIECE
E1 & F1	blue-black	16	3" x $3^1/2$"
E2	light blue	8	$1^1/2$" x 3"
F2	medium blue	8	$1^1/2$" x 3"

Remove the remaining paper, press, and set aside or place on the design wall.

Cutting Charts for Center Block 2

INNER ARC			
PLACEMENT	FABRIC	PIECES NEEDED	SIZE OF EACH PIECE
E1	medium blue	8	$1\frac{1}{2}$" x $4\frac{1}{2}$"
E2 & F1	blue-black	16	3" x $4\frac{1}{2}$"
F2	light blue	8	$1\frac{1}{2}$" x $4\frac{1}{2}$"

SPIKES BACKGROUNDS			
PLACEMENT	FABRIC	PIECES NEEDED	SIZE OF EACH PIECE
A1	pale yellow	8	$1\frac{3}{4}$" x $4\frac{1}{2}$"
A3	yellow	8	2" x $4\frac{1}{2}$"
A5	dark yellow	8	2" x $4\frac{1}{2}$"
A7	pale orange	8	3" x $4\frac{1}{2}$"
B2	orange	8	3" x $4\frac{1}{2}$"
B4	dark orange	8	2" x $4\frac{1}{2}$"
B6	orange-red	8	2" x $4\frac{1}{2}$"
B8	red-orange	8	$1\frac{3}{4}$" x $5\frac{1}{2}$"

SPIKES			
PLACEMENT	FABRIC	PIECES NEEDED	SIZE OF EACH PIECE
A2	dark purple	8	$1\frac{3}{4}$" x $4\frac{1}{2}$"
A4 & A6	purple	16	$1\frac{3}{4}$" x $4\frac{1}{2}$"
A8	light blue	8	$1\frac{3}{4}$" x $4\frac{1}{2}$"
B1	medium blue	8	$1\frac{3}{4}$" x $4\frac{1}{x}$"
B3 & B5	light purple	16	$1\frac{3}{4}$" x $4\frac{1}{2}$"
B7	lavender	8	$1\frac{3}{4}$" x $5\frac{1}{2}$"

OUTER ARC			
PLACEMENT	FABRIC	PIECES NEEDED	SIZE OF EACH PIECE
C1	orange	8	5" x $6\frac{1}{2}$"
C2	light blue	8	$1\frac{1}{2}$" x 4"
D1	medium blue	8	2" x 4"
D2	pale orange	8	5" x $6\frac{1}{2}$"

Piece as you did for block 1.

Do not join the halves of center block 2.

Cutting Charts for Outer Blocks

SPIKES AND BACKGROUND			
PLACEMENT	FABRIC	PIECES NEEDED	SIZE OF EACH PIECE
A1	*	16	$1\frac{1}{2}$" x $4\frac{1}{2}$"
A2	*	16	$1\frac{1}{2}$" x $4\frac{1}{2}$"
A5	*	16	$1\frac{1}{2}$" x $5\frac{1}{2}$"
A6	*	16	$1\frac{1}{2}$" x $5\frac{1}{2}$"
A8	*	16	$1\frac{1}{2}$" x 7"
B1	*	16	$1\frac{1}{2}$" x $4\frac{1}{2}$"
B2	*	16	$1\frac{1}{2}$" x $4\frac{1}{2}$"
B5	*	16	$1\frac{1}{2}$" x $5\frac{1}{2}$
B6	*	16	$1\frac{1}{2}$" x $5\frac{1}{2}$
B8	*	16	$1\frac{1}{2}$" x 7"
B9	*	16	$2\frac{1}{2}$" x 6"
A3 & B3	blue-black	32	$4\frac{1}{2}$" x $4\frac{1}{2}$"
A4 & B4	blue-black	32	$2\frac{1}{2}$" x 3"
A7 & B7	blue-black	32	3" x 5"

* I used all the gradations fabrics in the spikes, so I'm only giving the cutting sizes for those, not the specific fabrics. Cut a variety of the fabrics for each placement and have fun mixing them up in the blocks.

Paper piece the outer blocks. Join the halves.

Because the spikes are so long, don't be shy about using pins to keep your fabrics in place while you sew these blocks.

Setting Triangles

Starch the background yardage.

Cut 8 squares 6" x 6" twice on the diagonal for 32 side setting triangles.

Cut 2 squares $15\frac{1}{2}$" x $15\frac{1}{2}$" once on the diagonal for the corner triangles.

Cut 8 diamonds using the fire_diamond.pdf template (A).

Quilt Top Assembly

Start by assembling 1 section with a center block 1 with two halves of center block 2, two outer blocks, two side setting triangles, and one diamond. Make 8 sections.

Fig. 5. fireworks_assembly.pdf

See? Everything is on a nice square. No Y seams.

Sew two sections together and move around the quilt, assembling sections, then joining every two sections and so on. Finally, sew on the corner triangles and your quilt is complete.

OK, now you can say it. WOW!! Sometimes, when I get to this point, I just stand back and stare. I certainly did with this quilt. I couldn't believe it actually came out of my head. Don't be so surprised; I really think some of these quilts come from somewhere else. How could I possibly think these things up? Well, no matter, it's here now and we love it.

Borders

I chose to put on a thin inner border of 2" strips, cut lengthwise, just to break up the border from the body of the quilt. If you think yours will look better without the inner border, don't make it. It's OK to leave it off.

Foundations

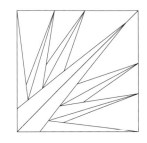

Fig. 6. Print 1 fire_bordercorner.pdf

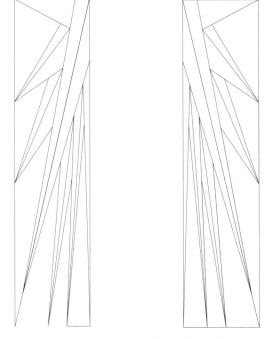

Fig. 7. Print 1 fire_border_a.pdf   Fig. 8. Print 1 fire_border_b.pdf

Cutting Chart for Border

In order to get the explosive look for the border, dig into your scraps for a random collection of bright fabrics—yellows, limes, reds, pinks, etc. Make sure they are all at least as large as the largest pieces needed and mix them up. That's the easiest way to work, making sure they're all big enough to go anywhere.

Placement	Fabric	Pieces Needed	Size of Each Piece
Border Blocks A & B			
A spikes	bright colors	12	1" x 18"
A background	blue-black	6	$2\frac{1}{2}$" x 12"
B1-B8 spikes	bright colors	10	$2\frac{1}{2}$" x $7\frac{1}{2}$"
B9 spikes	bright colors	2	$1\frac{1}{2}$" x 20"
B background	blue-black	6	$3\frac{1}{2}$" x 12"
Corner Block			
A & B spikes	bright colors	12	1" x $6\frac{1}{2}$"
A & B background	blue-black	6	2" x $4\frac{1}{2}$"

Cut 6 strips 2" wide for the inner border.
Cut 6 strips $4\frac{1}{2}$" wide for the outer border.

Paper piece the 2 border blocks and the corner. Use pins to stabilize the long pieces.

Square up the quilt and add the inner and outer borders as shown (fig. 9).

Wowee, huh? Now guess what we have to do? Yep...quilt it. Once again, it's a very personal decision, but I chose to continue the fireworks theme and quilt that in.

You can see what I did; now it's your turn. I'd love to see how you quilted yours!

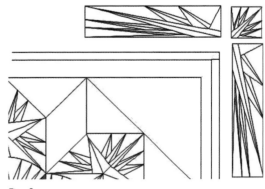

Fig. 9.

DREAM CATCHER

62" x 62", made by author

DREAM CATCHER came about quite by accident. I had just finished working on a very bright, bold quilt and needed something a bit more calming to work on. While I was designing this, I actually saw it in my head as a bright quilt, with lots of blue in it. Suffice it to say, it doesn't look anything like what I thought it would, but it's growing on me!

This quilt looks very intricate, but you will find as you piece it, it's really pretty simple. Sure, there are a lot of pieces, but cutting and stacking in advance really moves things right along, don't you think? This quilt does have some Y-seams. I know you're probably groaning now. I tried designing them out, but the quilt started looking too "seamy."

Yardage

5½ yards cream background
½ yard each of light yellow, yellow, dark yellow, navy blue, orange, purple, and brown
⅜ yard gold inner border
½ yard red inner border
¾ yard navy blue outer border
½ yard binding
4⅛ yards backing
70" x 70" batting

Foundations

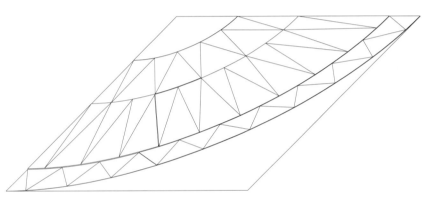

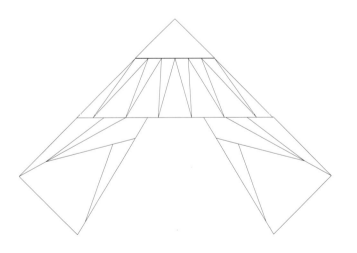

Fig. 1. Print 8 dream_center.pdf

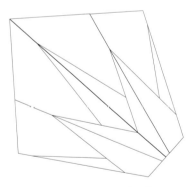

Fig. 3. Print 4 dream_crown_b.pdf

Fig. 2. Print 4 dream_crown_a.pdf

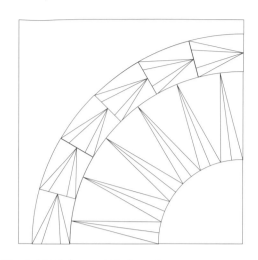

Fig. 4. Print 4 dream_chick_feet.pdf

Cutting

As with the other complex quilts, we'll do the cutting as we go along, although you are certainly free to do all the cutting at once. Just page through the pattern and pick out all the cutting charts. Just be sure to label your pieces.

Placement is indicated by foundation labels throughout.

Sewing Sequence

Assembling as you go along, start in the middle to eliminate any wonkiness or lumps at the center.

Cutting Chart for the Center Blocks

PLACEMENT	COLOR	PIECES NEEDED	SIZE OF EACH PIECE
B spikes	blue	40	2" x 4"
B background	cream	48	3" x 4"
C spikes	brown	40	2" x 6"
C background	cream	48	3" x 6"
D spikes	yellow	40	3" x 3"
D background	brown	48	3" x 3"

Starch the red and background yardage and cut 8 inside arcs (A) from the red fabric and 8 outside arcs (E) from the background fabric.

Paper piece the spikey inner arcs (B).

Ease on the plain inside arcs (A). Remove the paper.

Paper piece the middle 2 spikey arcs (C and D).

Ease the A/B units onto the C spikey arcs. Remove the paper.

Ease the A/B/C units onto the D spikey arcs.

Ease the plain outside arcs (E) onto the A/B/C/D units.

Remove all the paper. Press the blocks and set aside or place on your design wall.

Fig. 5. Center diamond block

Cutting Chart for the Chicken Feet Blocks

PLACEMENT	COLOR	PIECES NEEDED	SIZE OF EACH PIECE
B spikes	dark yellow	24	2" x 6"
B spikes	light yellow	24	2" x 6"
B background	cream	28	3" x 6
C-H chicken feet	navy blue	48	1½" x 4"
C-H background	cream	72	2" x 4"

Starch background fabric and cut out 4 inside arcs (A) and 4 outside arcs (I).

Paper piece the spikey inner arcs (B).

Ease the plain inside arcs (A) onto the spikey arcs (B). Remove the paper.

Paper piece chicken feet arcs (refer to the instructions in the PERFECT PLACEMAT pattern, page 27).

Ease on the outside arcs (I).

Join the two sections to complete the block, with the B unit on top and the chicken feet unit, still with the paper on, beneath.

Cutting Chart for the Crown Blocks

PLACEMENT	COLOR	PIECES NEEDED	SIZE OF EACH PIECE
B spikes	navy blue	24	2" x 5"
B background	cream	28	2½" x 5"
C-H crown back-ground	cream	32	4" x 8"
C-H light spikes	yellow	28	3" x 8"
C-H medium spikes	orange	16	3" x 8"
C-H dark spikes	purple	12	3" x 8"

Starch a 3½" strip of red fabric and cut out 4 inside triangles (A).

Paper piece the inner spikey units (B).

Join the B units with the inside triangles (A). Remove the paper.

Paper piece each segment of the crown, referring to the figure for color placement of the spikes (fig. 6).

Fig. 6. Crown block

Join the segments C through H. Add the inner unit. Remove all the paper. Press the blocks and set aside.

Add the chicken feet and crown blocks to the center unit as shown, using Y-seam construction. Stop stitching ¼" from the ends of the seams.

Fig. 7. Block assembly

As the quilt starts taking shape, I start thinking about quilting motifs. This is where they're born for me. I'll see areas that I want to quilt with certain motifs. When I got to this point, I already knew I wanted to do feathers somewhere...anywhere. For those of you who have met me, you know I'm *not* a feather person. My feathers resemble what you'd see a child draw, but I used a stencil and the feathers in the center came out just fine. You may envision something else there. Go for it!

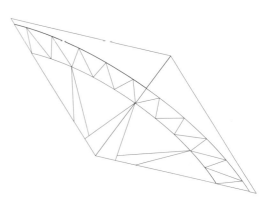
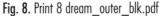

Fig. 8. Print 8 dream_outer_blk.pdf

Cutting Chart for the Outer Blocks

PLACEMENT	COLOR	PIECES NEEDED	SIZE OF EACH PIECE
A & B medium spikes	orange	16	2" x 6"
B light spikes	yellow	8	2½" x 6"
A dark spikes	purple	8	2½" x 6"
A & B background	cream	32	3" x 8"
C & D spikes	navy blue	80	2" x 2"
C & D background	cream	96	2" x 2"

Starch the background fabric and cut 8 each of the outside arcs (E and F).

Paper piece the inner spikey arcs (A and B). Join in pairs and remove the paper.

Paper piece the middle spikey arcs (C and D). Ease the inner and middle arcs together, with the inner arcs on top (A with D and B with C).

Ease the outside arcs on (F with A/D and E with B/C). Remove all the paper and press.

Fig. 8. Adding outer ring blocks

Join the blocks with the completed center as shown.

Cut 2 squares 15¾" x 15¾" in half on the diagonal. Sew them on as shown on page 91 to complete the inner quilt top.

Borders

The border blocks are constructed in halves, which are then joined.

Foundations

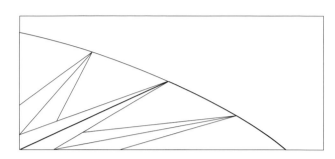

Fig. 9. Print 4 dream_border_a.pdf

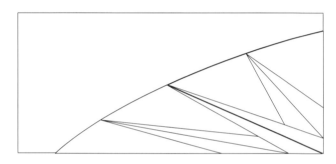

Fig. 10. Print 4 dream_border_b.pdf

Cutting Chart for the Spikey Border Blocks

PLACEMENT	COLOR	PIECES NEEDED	SIZE OF EACH PIECE
spikes background	cream	32	3½" x 6"
spikes	purple	24	1½" x 7"
spikes	orange	24	1½" x 7"
outside arc	navy blue	8	4½" x 10"

Cut 4 each of the two outside arcs (C and CR) from the navy blue fabric.

Cut 6 gold strips 1" wide for the first inner border.

Cut 6 red strips 1½" wide for the second inner border.

Cut 4 navy blue strips 5½" wide for the outer border.

Add the two inner borders to the quilt top.

Paper piece the inner arcs (A and B).

Join A/B pairs as shown.

Ease the outside arcs (C) onto the A/B pairs. Remove the paper.

Join mirror-image halves to complete the border blocks.

Cut the outer border strips in half and add to the ends of the 4 border blocks.

Trim to size and add to the quilt top.

Fig. 11. Quilt top assembly

Quilting

OK, here we are again, it's time for the quilting. I had fun on this one. As you can see, I drew some lizards (no comment on the drawing please) and quilted them in. I did an overall medium meander for the background with feathers in the center.

CHAPTER 6
TOOLS, TIPS, AND OTHER FUN STUFF

As quilters, we all have items we like, sewing machines that work for us, and of course we're authorities on our favorite tools (or so we'd like to think!).

I know that some folks would like to see what works for me and possibly take away some information or tidbit that will work for them as well. Standing in classrooms is the best way to find out what folks REALLY want to know—so here are some of the answers to those nagging questions.

Sewing Machine

First and foremost, folks ask about what I sew on. This question never ceases to make me smile. Purchasing a sewing machine is a very personal decision. It's really easy to just find out what others sew on and go buy the same thing, but will it be the machine for you?

I did a lot of test-driving on machines. I went from shop to shop, brought my own fabric and quilt sandwich, and sewed, and sewed, and sewed. I knew the machine had to "fit." It became a rather mind boggling experience and, I have to admit, the husband was getting a bit testy schlepping from shop to shop and waiting while I stitched.

Then I found my baby. I was teaching at the Paducah show and demonstrating my technique on the in-classroom machine. (Major sewing machine companies provide sewing machines for the students and teachers to use.) In my classroom we had the Brother® Innov-is QC-1000.

This machine did everything I wanted it to do (and way more)—she fit, she was comfortable, quiet, and purred for me. I knew this was the one. So that's what I have. I still adore her, and it's been a year now, so that's a good thing, no?

So, test drive, test drive, test drive. Make a list of must haves, wants, and wishes. Take the list with you and trust me, you will find your machine.

Paper

Since all these quilts are done with paper piecing, the paper you use is extremely important. I spent over a year trying different papers. Just as with sewing machines, paper CAN make a difference.

Newsprint is too flimsy for me. Working on blocks with a lot of pieces requires a lot of manipulation and newsprint can't stand up to that kind of abuse. Cheap typing paper is too linty, stiff, and opaque. It's a great, cheap fix, but not really good for our environment either. I felt that twang of guilt about the trees that were sacrificing their existence for me to sew.

I tried all different types of vegetable-based papers with no success. Then I found THE paper. It's cotton (no trees died in the making of this paper); it's vellum-like (has a perfect transparency for lining up fabrics); it's strong (to stand up to continued manipulation of complicated blocks); it tears away easily when done. Because it's cotton, the fibers are longer and the lint is minimal. The best part, though, is that it plays nicely with laser *and* inkjet printers. I use this exclusively. It's my product, so contact me and I'll tell you where to get it. (See Resources, page 94.)

Thread

You can go anywhere on the Internet and find discussions about threads. There are a lot of thread manufacturers out there, but in my opinion some are clearly ahead of the pack.

With paper piecing, the seams are not pressed open, so you need a thin and strong thread that won't contribute to the bulk of a seam. Finding one that works well in the top and bobbin is not always as easy as it sounds. But I found one that I think is extraordinary.

For all of my piecing now, I use WonderFil® Deco Bob thread. It comes in exquisite neutrals that work wonderfully well with darks and lights. I just finished a black-and-white quilt and you literally can *not* see the thread at all. How much better can you get than that? Also, my seams feel almost completely flat with this thread. No bulk at all. Luscious!

For quilting, I use tons and tons of different threads. They are all either from Superior Threads or WonderFil. Those are my two favorite thread companies. I adore metallics, silks, rayons, cottons—any threads that sing on my quilts. I know some of you don't find this very helpful, but just as with fabric, you have to play with them to see what works for you.

Fabrics

For the most part I sew exclusively with batiks. Why? Why not! I like the hand, weight, and drape of batiks. They work extraordinarily well with paper piecing. Their depth of color, scrumptious patterns, and overall appeal don't hurt either! This too, is a very personal decision.

Tools

The number one, most important tool you can own when paper piecing is the Add-A-Quarter™ ruler. It comes in two sizes: six inches and 12 inches long. Get both. I also use the Add-an-Eighth™ ruler for those blocks with a zillion pieces. These rulers are simply must-have items.

My last favorite tool is my seam roller. I use a wooden seam roller and it's saved me from countless burns from my iron. I tend to grab without looking when I'm in the "sew zone," and irons can be dangerous (just ask my right hand), so I came up with using the seam roller for pressing seams as I go along. Love it, love it, love it!

Rotary cutters and mats are in that area of personal decision, but the Olfa® cutter with the handle you squeeze to make the blade come out is my choice. It's ergonomic, comfortable, and safe. I got rid of all my other cutters (see my left hand for the reasons why).

I'm extremely opinionated about machine needles, too. I only use embroidery and topstitch needles. I find they are the needles that work the best with paper piecing and my quilting. I have found they tend to stay sharp the longest and sew the best with paper piecing.

Batting

There are some absolutely luscious batts out there designed for a plethora of uses. Since the majority of my quilts are for the wall, I need to choose batts that work well with wall art. My favorites are Hobbs Tuscany Silk, Tuscany Wool, Tuscany Poly, and Tuscany 80/20 cotton/poly. I rotate among these, depending on what I'm trying to achieve with each individual quilt.

I use the silk on high-end bed quilts. It's beautifully drapey. The wool gives me the flattest, lightest weight, most delicious wallhangings. The poly has a higher loft and I use it for baby quilts. (Parents want fluffy!) Finally, the cotton/poly is my all-purpose batting that I use for everything else.

Starch

I have started using starch like a madwoman. Why? Quite by accident, actually. I had to rip out an arc on one of my quilts twice (I never said I was a quick learner!) and saw that it was getting kind of limp from all the sewing and ripping. So I grabbed some starch and gave the piece back some life. It sewed on perfectly.

Then, of course, I had to play with different starches. I kept hearing that if you starch, bugs would dine on your quilts. That didn't exactly excite me, so I needed to find a "dine-free" version of starch. I found one *and* it smells divine! I use Mary Ellen's Best Press (the Caribbean Beach flavor) and it's awesome—crisp, flake free, aromatic, and in an environmentally sound container. It's a great product. Try it. (See Resources.)

Quilting

I'm always asked if I do my own quilting. The simple answer is yes, but I didn't always do my own.

When I first started, I sent my quilts out because I was sure I couldn't possibly do that myself. But I can. You can, too! I find that to be my favorite part of the process now, so I urge you to give it a try.

What do I quilt on? That depends. My small quilts (40" and under) get quilted on my domestic machine. Anything larger goes onto my Handi Quilter.

Why Handi Quilter? That's easy; it's without a doubt, my all-time favorite mid- to longarm setup. Just like my sewing machine, I test drove all the machines out there. I felt like Goldilocks. Some were too loud, others had too much vibration, and some just didn't play well with threads.

I use a lot of different types of threads in

my quilting and simply must have a machine that can handle them all. The HQ Sixteen is that machine. It's quiet (I can actually hear my TV while I'm quilting), it simply floats over the quilts with no drag whatsoever, and it *really* plays well with all the threads I've ever tried on it. I also think it's the most machine you can or ever will find for the money. OK...OK...I'm biased, but try this machine—I bet you'll agree!

So these are the tools that I use. I consider them my assistants and friends when I'm working. If one is gone, things don't go as well as planned. I always make sure I have all my tools ready for every project!

Of course, I'm always trying new things, too, so if you have tips or tools you think are must haves, I'd love to know about them!

RESOURCES

Brother
www.brother-usa.com
for my favorite sewing machine

Electric Quilt
www.electricquilt.com
for EQ® software and more

Handi Quilter
www.handiquilter.com
for the best home machine quilting systems available

Mary Ellen
www.maryellenproducts.com
for Mary Ellen's Best Press® spray starch, my favorite

QuiltMavens' Perfect Paper Piecing Paper
www.quiltmavens.com
for translucent foundation paper and wooden seam rollers

ABOUT THE AUTHOR

Who's Deb?

They said I needed a bio. Apparently there's someone out there who wants to read this page, so have fun!

I've been married to the same guy for 35 years (oy vey).

I have two grown daughters, and even though I live in the age of 60-year-old mothers, I have no plans of having any more kids.

I'm a very proud grammy of 4 (so far!) grandkids (triplets by one daughter and a darling little guy by the other daughter).

My favorite color is red but I rarely use it in quilts. What's up with that?

I try to design at least one quilt a day. Really.

I enter quilts into shows to see them hanging up. I don't have a lot of large wall space in my home.

I am blessed to have received numerous international, national, and local awards for my quilts and I never even had to bribe one single person! You've gotta love that.

I'm owned by two Devon Rex cats, Elvis and Minkee.

I live in San Francisco, mostly for the weather, the restaurants, the ocean, the views, the cosmopolitan feel the city has and, of course, the earthquakes.

I have no formal art training. I can't draw a straight line.

I've been told I need to take color appreciation classes. (I'm very confused by this, because I appreciate color…I really do!)

I'm constantly told that I do things wrong in quilting (i.e., piecing techniques, binding, appliqué). I don't care, it works for me.

I firmly believe that life is too short, so just do it. Don't think about what you COULD be doing, SHOULD be doing, or WOULD have done…just do it. I did and you're reading it! Oh..and it should be fun.

So, if you're still not bored senseless, join me on my online group through Yahoo… debkarasikquilts!

Deb

For todays quilters...
inspiration and creativity from AQS Publishing

7601
us $26.95

7611
us $26.95

7605
us $24.95

7018
us $24.95

7922
us $26.95

7772
us $26.95

LOOK for these books nationally.   **CALL** or **VISIT** our Web site at

1-800-626-5420 • www.AmericanQuilter.com